ALTHEA GIBSON

Tom Biracree

MELROSE SQUARE PUBLISHING COMPANY
LOS ANGELES, CALIFORNIA

Senior Consulting Editor for Chelsea House
Nathan Irvin Huggins
Director
W.E.B. Du Bois Institute for Afro-American Research
Harvard University

Consulting Editor for Melrose Square
Raymond Friday Locke

Cover Painting: Jesse S. Santos
Cover Design: Jeff Renfro

ALTHEA
GIBSON

MELROSE SQUARE BLACK AMERICAN SERIES

ELLA FITZGERALD
singer

NAT TURNER
slave revolt leader

PAUL ROBESON
singer and actor

JACKIE ROBINSON
baseball great

LOUIS ARMSTRONG
musician

SCOTT JOPLIN
composer

MATTHEW HENSON
explorer

MALCOLM X
militant black leader

CHESTER HIMES
author

SOJOURNER TRUTH
antislavery activist

CONTENTS

Chapter One

Lightning Strikes Forest Hills

O N A GRAY September morning in 1950, Althea Gibson left the Harlem home of her friend Rhoda Smith and boarded a New York City subway train. She rode the D train downtown to Rockefeller Center and transferred to the F train, which would take her across the East River from Manhattan to Queens. Carrying a gym bag and 2 tennis rackets, the tall, lanky 23 year old looked like any young woman out for a day of exercise. But anxiety gripped Gibson as she sat on the train, for the most important day of her career lay before her. The tennis player was on her way to the

Althea Gibson's brilliant performance at the 1950 U.S. National Tennis Championships at Forest Hills broke the racial barrier in tournament tennis.

West Side Tennis Club in Forest Hills to compete in the second round of the U.S. National Tennis Championships.

Gibson had ample reason to feel nervous. A newcomer to Forest Hills, she was about to face a seasoned opponent: Louise Brough, the 1947 U.S. national champion, who had won her third straight Wimbledon title—the English national championship—that summer. Because of Brough's stature, the two women would play on the club's main court, in a

The West Side Tennis Club in Forest Hills (pictured) had hosted the U.S. tennis championship for 35 years before blacks were permitted to play there.

stadium packed with thousands of tennis fans, journalists, and celebrities. "I could hardly ask for a better opportunity to show what I could do," Gibson later wrote of the match. Still, she expected that the gallery might be less than friendly to her. She knew that some of the spectators did not believe she belonged on the

Louise Brough (above), three-time Wimbledon victor and 1947 U.S. national champion, had to call upon all her athletic skill to hold off the unexpectedly powerful Gibson.

clubhouse court, much less at the U.S. Nationals. It made no difference to them that she had proven her qualifications as an athlete again and again in preliminary tournaments. All that mattered to Althea Gibson's critics was that she was black.

Gibson had made her way to the national championship against all odds. Growing up poor in the rough neighborhood of Harlem, she never even played tennis until just before her 14th birthday. When she started competing, she was limited to tournaments sponsored by the black American Tennis Association (ATA). Gibson soon established herself as the best woman player in the ATA, racking up a string of 10 straight singles championships in 1947. Eager to test herself against other athletes of her own caliber, she felt frustrated by her exclusion from the whites-only United States Lawn Tennis Association (USLTA).

Before Althea Gibson arrived on the scene, only one black, a doctor named Reginald Weir, had ever entered a USLTA event. Unfortunately, his only appearance in 1947, had been disappointing and thus failed to break the racial barrier in tennis. But in 1950 Gibson had managed to gain admission to several USLTA tournaments, where her remarkable performances left no doubt that she deserved a chance to compete for the national championship. After heated debate in the tennis world, Gibson finally gained a slot at Forest Hills. But disgruntled officials relegated her to Court 14—situated inconveniently far from the clubhouse—for the first round of play. While movie star Ginger Rogers played a polite, if dull, mixed doubles match on the clubhouse court, Gibson was scrutinized by hordes of curious reporters and photographers during her match against Barbara Knapp of England.

Despite the disruptions and pressures, Gibson had won the first round and advanced to the next. Now, as the tennis player arrived at the West Side Tennis Club for a second day of competition, she saw spectators, undeterred by the day's gloomy weather, crowding into the stadium. The press, sensing headlines in the making, had also come out in force to watch the rookie do battle with the champion. Gibson, her stomach knotted with tension, could not eat lunch. When the time came for her match to start, she stepped onto the court looking "scared to death," according to one reporter.

The match got off to a predictable start as Brough confidently took game after game from a jumpy Gibson. At least one heckler made the first set harder on Gibson, shouting "Knock her out of there!" to Brough from the stands. Brough won the set quickly, six games

After a thunderstorm put a dramatic stop to their second-round match, Brough and Gibson met an excited corps of journalists to discuss the tournament.

to one. But as Gibson's prospects for victory grew more remote, her determination to win grew stronger. She hammered her way into the second set. Comparing Gibson's approach to the style of another tennis great, reporter

David Eisenberg of the *New York Journal American* wrote: "Rarely since Alice Marble's championship reign has a woman shown so much stroking power as [Gibson] did, especially with her forehand." Gibson took the set from her unwary competitor with a score of 6-3.

Neither Brough nor anyone in the crowd had expected Gibson to come this far. The audience fell silent as the two players launched into the third and deciding set under ever more threatening skies. Brough, edgy and defensive, struggled to rebuff the younger player's attacks while Gibson, aggressive and persistent, fought for every point. The champion prevailed for the first three games of the set, but her challenger only played harder. Tirelessly slashing away at Brough's lead, Gibson began taking games. Brough countered with wins of her own, evening up the score. But Gibson refused to give in, and by the end of the set's 13th game she had pulled ahead. The score stood at 7-6. Gibson needed only one more game to take the set and win the match.

Lightning flashed across the menacingly dark sky as Brough prepared to serve. The tennis star was "obviously very tired," wrote David Eisenberg. "The courage and power of this unknown . . . had robbed Louise of her poise. Everyone in the stands sensed that a fabulous upset was in the making. But it never came about. Ten minutes of thunder and lightning finally delivered the deluge." A torrential downpour sent spectators, officials, and competitors scrambling for cover. Lightning struck one corner of the stadium, toppling an enormous concrete eagle that had stood there for years. Rain drenched the court and the stands, making further play impossible. The USLTA postponed the rest of the match until the next morning.

Now the stress of the tournament began to take its toll. Shouting questions, reporters mobbed Gibson under the marquee. The young player, drained and dazed, fumbled for answers. Some bystanders tried to help her escape the crush, touching off arguments with the press. Gibson finally extracted herself from the crowd, fled the clubhouse, and took the subway back to Rhoda Smith's house on 154th Street to wait out the evening.

"There is no doubt in my mind, or in anybody else's," Gibson later wrote, "that the delay was the worst thing that could have happened to me. It gave me the whole evening—and the next morning, too, for that matter—to think about the match." Not only did the break in play allow Gibson's anxiety to return, it also robbed her of a crucial advantage over Brough. Gibson's relentless and unexpected-

ly strong challenge had worn Brough down, both physically and mentally, but the postponement of the match gave her time to rest and regain her composure.

The next day, recalled Gibson, "by the time I got through reading the morning papers I was a nervous wreck." She headed out to Forest Hills early, to warm up and try to relax. Sarah Palfrey Cooke, another USLTA player,

Despite wholehearted effort on the second day of her match against Brough, the anxious Gibson could not block the triumph of her more experienced opponent.

practiced with her, but Gibson noted that she was "still on edge" when she stepped out onto the clubhouse court again. The capacity crowd in the stadium included a huge press contingent eager to record the end of the history-making match. Serving in the first game, Brough quickly took a 40-0 lead. Gibson came back, almost evening the score, before Brough won the game to tie the set, 7-7.

"The next game was the best," Gibson later wrote. She had the serve but fell behind 15-40 before rallying to bring the score to deuce (40-40). To win the game now, one of the players would have to pull ahead by two points. Gibson gained a one-point advantage, then Brough, then Gibson again. The 2 women played 18 points before Brough claimed the game. Leading eight games to seven, Brough needed to win only one more game to take the set and the match. On her own serve, she soon led Gibson 40-15. If she could capture one more point, the match would be hers. Gibson stopped her once, bringing the score to 40-30, but then hit a backhand shot out of court. Brough took the third set, 9-7, winning the match. That morning's play had taken only 11 minutes.

Gibson, of course, was disappointed at the outcome of the match. "Believe me," she wrote, "it was a long ride back to Harlem on the subway that afternoon." But despite her loss, Gibson had earned a place in the USLTA. No one could deny that she had championship potential; no one could claim that she did not deserve a chance to prove herself again. The talent and commitment that produced her outstanding performance at the U.S. National Championships had established Gibson's right to compete against top tennis players. And she would go on to do so, eventually winning the 1958. For two years she would reign as the best female tennis player in the world.

Gibson's achievement would make it easier for other black competitors to enter world-class tennis events. After her 1950 appearance at the West Side Tennis Club, racists could no longer exclude blacks from tennis. Lightning had indeed struck Forest Hills that September day, in the form of a determined young athlete named Althea Gibson. Tennis would never be the same again.

Chapter Two

"I Always Wanted to Be Somebody"

ALTHEA GIBSON WAS born on August 25, 1927, in the small rural town of Silver, South Carolina. The eldest child of Daniel and Annie Gibson, she spent the first three years of her life on a cotton farm, where her sharecropper parents struggled to make ends meet. The family, along with one of Althea's uncles, lived in a small cabin and farmed a five-acre plot of land. In return for use of the cabin and land, they paid a portion of their crop to the owner of the farm. What they kept, they sold to pay for food and farm supplies. Sharecropping offered a meager living even

Children play in a vacant Harlem lot. Growing up in the poor, mostly black New York City neighborhood, Althea Gibson preferred the streets to the schoolroom.

in good years, but when the crop failed three years in a row because of bad weather, the Gibsons fell on even harder times. In 1930, when the nationwide economic collapse known as the Great Depression caused the price of cotton to fall to record lows, Althea's family earned only $75 for an entire year's work.

Like many poor southern blacks during the depression, the Gibsons looked north for op-

Sharecroppers gather cotton in the fields surrounding their home. Althea's parents were sharecroppers in Silver, South Carolina, during the first three years of her life.

portunity. Unemployment plagued the entire country, but there still seemed to be hope of finding work in cities like Chicago, New York, and Detroit. When Annie Gibson's sister Sally Washington came south from New York to attend another sister's funeral, Althea's parents decided to send the three year old to live in New York City with her. Daniel Gibson followed a few months later and quickly found a job as a handyman in a garage for $10 a week. To the Gibsons this was "big money." It allowed Annie Gibson to join Daniel and Althea almost immediately.

Daniel Gibson's income, however, could not cover the cost of an apartment, so the family moved in with Sally Washington, who lived in Harlem. Washington "did all right for herself," Althea Gibson later wrote in her autobiography, *I Always Wanted to Be Somebody*. Ever since the Eighteenth Amendment to the Constitution, ratified in 1919, had outlawed the sale of alcoholic beverages in the United States, Washington had sold bootleg whiskey out of her apartment. Her business brought in a substantial income, but it created an unstable environment in which to raise children.

Althea's uncles and their friends frequently stopped by the apartment to purchase whiskey, and sometimes they offered to take Althea off her mother's hands for an afternoon. "Naturally they would always end up drinking whiskey," Gibson related in her autobiography. "So would I. They gave it to me in a water glass, and without any water in it, either." The little girl ended up drunk more than once. Prohibition was repealed in 1933, when Althea was six, but the at-

A poster celebrates the legalization of alcoholic beverages. Before Prohibition was repealed, Althea lived with an aunt who sold whiskey illegally from her apartment.

mosphere in Sally Washington's apartment did not change. Concerned about their daughter, the Gibsons sent her to Philadelphia to live with another aunt, Daisy Kelly, "when I was about seven or eight," according to Gibson. The change of scene had little effect on mischievous Althea, who gave her aunt "plenty of trouble" for the next two years.

When Althea was nine she returned to New York to live with her parents, who had moved into an apartment of their own on West 143rd Street in Harlem. By now the family included three more girls—Millie, Annie, and Lillian—and a boy named Daniel. Althea's siblings were well behaved, but as she got older she started "getting into real trouble. . . I didn't like people telling me what to do," she recalled. A chronic truant, she missed more days of school than she attended. When in school, she frequently caused disruptions and was punished or suspended. At home she was disobedient and took countless whippings from her father.

"Sometimes I would be scared to go home," Gibson wrote of that period. "I would go to the police station on 135th Street and tell them that I was afraid to go home because my father was going to beat me up." This only made Daniel Gibson angrier, and things got harder for Althea. But discipline seemed to have a reverse effect on the rebellious girl: The more she received, the more defiant she became. She stole food from stands on the street, played hooky to go to the movies, and once stole a bicycle and sold it. If her mother gave her money to buy groceries for the family, Althea would often forget about the errand, join in a street game with her friends, and use the money for her own dinner. She frequently stayed away from home for days at a time to avoid punishment, which would be all the harsher for her absence.

Gibson wrote that she learned to take her father's lashings in stride. "When he would whip me," she recalled, "I would never . . . give him the satisfaction of crying." Eventually Daniel Gibson gave up on corporal punishment. If Althea insisted on spending her time in the streets, he decided, she might as well know how to protect herself. He taught her how to box, and the training proved invaluable. "Harlem is a mean place to grow up in," noted Gibson. As she grew older, Althea had to defend herself—and sometimes her family— against various bullies and gang members.

Once, she found one of her uncles "lolling on the stairs" of Sally Washington's apartment building, "slightly intoxicated." A leader of a local gang, the Sabres, was in the process of robbing him. Althea pushed the boy aside and helped her uncle up, but the boy threw a sharpened screwdriver at her, gashing her hand. After removing her uncle from harm's way, Althea "went back down after that boy and we had a fight that they still talk about on 144th Street. We fought all over the block." The combatants fought to a draw and "were both pretty bloody and bruised" before some adults broke it up. After that, according to Gibson, no one in Harlem "ever tried to use me for a dart board again."

Althea's skill as a fighter reflected the competitiveness and athletic ability that made her a familiar figure on Harlem's playgrounds. In the summer, on weekends, and on the many days that she skipped school, she spent most of her time bowling or playing basketball, baseball, or paddle tennis. "The only thing I really liked to do was play ball," she wrote. Althea enjoyed sports partly because she excelled at each one she tried. Using worn-out or improvised equipment on makeshift courts, alleys, or fields, she discovered and developed her talents. As she did, she found a sense of self-worth that eluded her at home and in school. "The main reason why I hated to go to school," she revealed, "was because I couldn't see any point in wasting all that time that I could be spending shooting baskets in the playground." The time she spent playing sports brought her not only self-confidence but also medals and trophies won in city-sponsored competitions. On the playground Althea felt like somebody. And on the playground, she got her first chance to become somebody.

In the summer of 1941, at the age of 13, Althea graduated from junior high school. She spent the lazy days that followed on the playgrounds and streets of Harlem, taking part in whatever sports she found going on. Because of the shortage of open space in Harlem, New York City set aside some of the neighborhood's streets as "play streets" and employed adults to supervise activity there. On one such block of West 143rd Street, the city had set up a paddle-tennis court about half the size of a standard tennis court, where people came to play a game similar to tennis using wooden paddles. Althea stopped by the court one July day and challenged another player to a match. Buddy Walker, a musician known as Harlem's Society Orchestra Leader, was moonlighting as the block play leader that day, and his ability to spot athletic talent changed Althea Gibson's life.

As Walker watched Althea play, he was struck with the idea that she might be able to play regular tennis as well as she played paddle tennis. He talked it over with her, bought two secondhand rackets for five dollars apiece, and took her to nearby Mount Morris Park to hit tennis balls against the wall of the handball court. "Buddy got very excited about how well I hit the ball," Gibson recounted in her autobiography. He arranged to take her to the Harlem River Tennis Courts so she could try her hand at the real thing. A few days later

Althea met Walker there and played several games against one of his friends. Her natural talent for the game was so obvious that "a lot of the other players on the courts stopped their games to watch me," Gibson recalled.

One of those players was Juan Serrell, a

During the 1920s and 1930s the Cotton Club (shown) was part of the vibrant culture that thrived in Harlem alongside poverty and crime.

teacher who belonged to the Cosmopolitan Club, New York's most prestigious black tennis club. He was so impressed with Althea's performance that he made arrangements for her to play with the Cosmopolitan Club's professional "so that everybody could see what

I could do," Gibson wrote. Before a small crowd of Cosmopolitan Club members, Althea played a few sets against Fred Johnson. "Everybody thought I looked like a real good prospect," Gibson noted. "They took up a collection and bought me a membership." She began taking regular lessons from Johnson.

The members of the Cosmopolitan Club were interested in Althea because they were looking for ways to promote the participation of blacks in tennis. Ever since its creation in 1873, lawn tennis had been a country club sport, played almost exclusively by the wealthy. Few blacks had the opportunity to learn the sport, because blacks were excluded from the country clubs where it was played. Only a handful of segregated country clubs and public courts were open to those blacks who wanted—and could afford—to play tennis. As a result, whites dominated the sport.

In most of the tennis-playing world—most notably the United States, Great Britain, France, and Australia—the tournaments that served as the proving grounds for the best players were sponsored by white country clubs. Only white players could compete at these clubs. Black players were limited to black country clubs and the tournaments they held. Barred from the major tournaments, black players had no way to establish their legitimacy as competitive tennis players on a par with whites.

Black country clubs, such as the Cosmopolitan Club, formed the American Tennis Association (ATA) to regulate competition among black tennis players, much as the United States Lawn Tennis Association (USLTA) governed play among whites. But many black tennis players hoped to break the racial barrier that divided the sport. Althea Gibson's sponsors at the Cosmopolitan Club saw in the young woman a potential champion who might be able to achieve this goal.

At the Cosmopolitan Club, Althea discovered a whole new world. Her benefactors, she wrote, were "the highest class of Harlem people and they had rigid ideas about what was socially acceptable behavior." The game of tennis was itself very formal, with strict codes of etiquette and dress. Althea, accustomed to doing as she pleased, resisted the discipline at first, but then "began to understand that you could walk out onto the court . . . all dressed up in immaculate white, be polite to everybody, and still play like a tiger." As she accepted the rules of the game, her ability as an athlete developed.

Off the court, however, Althea "was still living pretty wild." She had dropped out of high school, left home briefly to live in a children's shelter, and taken a series of menial jobs to earn spending money. Unable to accept the restrictions of living at the shelter, she reluctantly returned home; unable to accept the responsibilities of a job, she gave up working. "I just stayed away from home and bummed around the streets" every day and most nights, Gibson recalled. Finally the city welfare department caught up with her, rented a room for her with a stable family, and put her on an allowance. "The hardest work I did," she wrote of this period, "aside from practicing tennis, was to report to the Welfare ladies once a week . . . and pick up my allowance."

Gradually, as Althea became more involved in tennis, her personal life grew more orderly. She began to take the game more seriously when she saw Alice Marble, winner of Wimbledon and the U.S. National Championships, play an exhibition match at the Cosmopolitan Club in 1942. "I can still remember saying to myself, boy, would I like to be able to play tennis like that!" Gibson later remarked. Marble's power and aggressiveness on the court showed Althea, she wrote, "possibilities in the game of tennis that I had never seen before." The young woman set her sights on becoming the best tournament player she could be. Althea's game developed quickly, and a year after she started lessons with

When tennis was introduced in the late 19th century, it was played only by the wealthy white members of exclusive country clubs.

Fred Johnson, he entered her in her first tournament, the ATA's New York State Open Championship, held at the Cosmopolitan Club. She won the tournament, writing later that she "was a little surprised about winning, but not much." Her victory "softened a lot of opinions" that the genteel Cosmopolitan Club membership had about the streetwise Althea. She had demonstrated her merit as a tennis player and proven herself worthy of the club's support.

Barred from white tennis clubs, blacks interested in the sport had to form their own organizations, such as the New York Tennis Association (shown here).

Later that summer Althea's sponsors sent her to the ATA's national girls' championship at Lincoln University in Pennsylvania. She made it all the way to the final before losing. Althea's performance showed that her tennis game had come a long way. But her tennis etiquette still needed some work. Nana Davis, the player who defeated her in the final, later commented that "Althea was a very crude creature. . . . After I beat her, she headed straight for the grandstand without bother-

Althea saw Alice Marble (above) play an exhibition match at the Cosmopolitan Club. Marble won the U.S. national championship four times and the British championship once.

ing to shake hands. Some kid had been laughing at her and she was going to throw him out."

Over the next four years a few new people entered Althea's world and began to smooth her rough edges. As she continued working on her tennis game at the Cosmopolitan Club, a member named Rhoda Smith took Althea under her wing and taught her proper tennis decorum. By the time Althea competed in the 1944 ATA championships (the 1943 tournament was canceled because of World War II), her manners had improved markedly. She won the 1944 girls' division title and repeated her success in 1945.

When Althea turned 18 in August 1945, her life changed. Because she was no longer a minor, she could not receive welfare support. She had to find a new place to live and start earning her own keep. Althea took a job as a waitress and moved in with her best friend, Gloria Nightingale, who lived with her family in Harlem. "I was able to run my own life at last," recalled Gibson. She and Gloria spent their evenings bowling and playing basketball, sometimes staying out until three or four in the morning. "Gloria was like me," Gibson wrote. "All she cared about was playing games and having a good time." Soon, however, a new influence in Althea's life inspired her to start

thinking about the future.

One evening in a bowling alley, Gloria introduced Althea to Sugar Ray Robinson and his wife, Edna Mae Robinson. At the time, Robinson was a young boxer competing in the

Sugar Ray Robinson and his wife, Edna Mae (right), befriended Althea in 1945. Robinson urged Althea to get an education and pursue a tennis career.

welterweight class. Already a local celebrity, he would achieve international fame in December 1946 when he won the world welterweight boxing title. His career would include five world championships in the middleweight class and would make him one of the most admired athletes of his day. The Robinsons liked Althea instantly and took an immediate interest in her welfare. "They seemed to understand that I needed a whole lot of help," Gibson wrote.

Althea began spending most of her free time with the couple, often sleeping in their apartment and accompanying them on trips to the country, where Sugar Ray Robinson trained. Althea thrived on the attention and affection they gave her and took Sugar Ray Robinson as her role model. "I worshiped Sugar Ray Robinson . . . because he was somebody," Gibson recalled. "I was determined that I was going to be somebody—if it killed me." The Robinsons encouraged Althea to make the most of her talents, and the young athlete took their advice to heart. In 1946, Althea moved from the girls' division to the women's division of ATA competition. At the championships that year she reached the final but lost to Roumania Peters, who had won the women's title in 1944. "I was overconfident, there's no doubt about it," she explained. She later considered the loss a "good lesson." Althea's defeat disappointed some of her sponsors, but her performance impressed two doctors involved in promoting black tennis players. Drs. Hubert A. Eaton and Robert W.

Johnson approached Althea and offered to help her gain admission to college, where she could, in her words, "get an education and improve my tennis at the same time." They were shocked to learn that Althea was a high school dropout.

After discussing the situation with ATA officials, Eaton and Johnson presented Althea with a proposal. She could live with Dr. Eaton and his family in Wilmington, North Carolina, during the school year, attend high school, and practice her tennis on his court. In the summer she could live with Dr. Johnson's family in Lynchburg, Virginia, and travel with him to ATA tournaments. Althea felt ambivalent about their offer. She knew she wasn't getting anywhere in Harlem, but moving away and returning to school would turn her life upside down.

"Harlem wasn't heaven but at least I knew I could take care of myself there," she wrote. Althea had heard terrifying stories about the South. But agreeing to the doctors' plan would allow Althea to find out just how far she could go in tennis. Finally, Sugar Ray and Edna Mae Robinson convinced Althea to accept the offer. Just after her 19th birthday, Althea Gibson boarded a train at Pennsylvania Station in Manhattan and headed south.

Chapter Three

Southern Sojourn

ALTHEA GIBSON STEPPED down from the train and stood on the platform of the Wilmington, North Carolina, train station. In each hand she carried a tattered cardboard suitcase tied shut with spare belts, and from a strap around her neck hung a saxophone given her by Sugar Ray Robinson. The "tired old skirt" she wore had been wrinkled on the overnight ride from New York, and Gibson herself was exhausted from sitting up for the entire sleepless journey. She had spent most of the trip "worrying about how it would be" in the South, wondering "whether I would like

At the age of 19, Gibson moved to Wilmington, North Carolina, to attend high school. She spent most of her free time there working on her tennis game.

it living with the family . . . would the movie houses refuse to let me in because I was colored, would I have to get off the sidewalk if a white person came along." When she arrived at her destination, she was "as nervous as a cat."

Gibson's attack of nerves subsided when the Eaton family's chauffeur approached her and introduced himself. Soon the young woman from Harlem was being driven to her new home in the back seat of a big car. "This shouldn't be too hard to take," she thought. Things looked just as good when she arrived at the Eatons' house. Mrs. Eaton greeted Althea warmly, pointed out her room, and told her to feel at home. After fixing herself a meal of bacon and eggs, Gibson took a look around. "It was a far cry from what I'd been used to," she later wrote of the Eaton residence. A full-time maid kept the spacious, tastefully furnished house immaculate. A carefully maintained tennis court was a prominent feature of the large yard. In more ways than one, Wilmington was a long way from Harlem.

The Eatons took Gibson into their family in every way. They not only gave her a place to stay and practice her tennis, they also bought her clothes and gave her an allowance. In return, Dr. and Mrs. Eaton expected Gibson to follow the same rules as their own children.

At the age of 19, having grown accustomed over the years to living on her own, Gibson had to adjust to a highly structured family life. She later noted in her autobiography that "nobody stayed out all night in that house, or decided

A billboard in New York City (above) decries racial and religious prejudice. While living in the South, Gibson missed the more tolerant atmosphere of the North.

to eat lunch in a dog wagon downtown instead of coming home for lunch with the family." She found the routine difficult to accept at first but gradually got used to it, knowing it was a small price to pay for the opportunity Dr. Eaton was giving her.

Gibson also had to get used to the discipline of school. It had been almost five years since she last stepped foot in a classroom, and she dreaded the prospect of spending the next four years studying. Even though her spotty academic record only qualified her for the seventh grade in the local school system, she was determined to enter high school as a sophomore and graduate in three years. School administrators gave Gibson an aptitude test to determine the grade in which she belonged. Her score qualified her to start as a sophomore, with the provision that she could be dropped back if her performance was unsatisfactory. Eager to finish school as quickly as possible, she "buckled down to [her] schoolwork like nobody's business." Although the freewheeling Gibson sometimes resented the restrictions of her new life, she understood that cooperation would benefit her in the long run. Her move to Wilmington, however, also imposed other limits on her freedom, limits that deprived her of basic human rights. In Wilmington, as throughout the rest of the

On her first bus ride in Wilmington, Gibson encountered the law requiring blacks to sit in the rear. The experience made her "feel ashamed."

southern United States, overt racial discrimination was legally sanctioned. Blacks were barred from the best employment, housing, and educational opportunities and were forbidden to eat in certain restaurants, use public recreational facilities, or seek medical care in many hospitals. They were required to drink from "colored only" water fountains, sit in the rear of buses, and use the back balconies of movie theaters. In parts of the South, it was illegal for blacks and whites to play tennis together, even on a private court. The segregation laws reflected a pervasive racism that often had even crueler, and sometimes deadly, effects on the life of southern blacks, sometimes taking the form of beatings and lynchings.

Gibson, of course, was no stranger to racial discrimination. In New York City she had seen the impact of equally pernicious, if more subtle, forms of racism. The slightly better job opportunities enjoyed by northern blacks and the absence of segregation laws could not make up for dismal living conditions in crowded ghettos such as Harlem, which was ravaged by crime, gang warfare, unemployment, and drug and alcohol abuse. But, perhaps because southern racism took the form of laws that Gibson did not want to obey, the independent young woman found the situation in the South particularly offensive. The meaning of segregation came into sharp focus for Gibson the first time she rode a bus in Wilmington. Posted on board was a sign that read: White in Front, Colored in Rear. "I was burned up that I had to conform to such an ignorant law," she later recalled. With her typical rebelliousness, she chose a seat "as near to the front as I thought I could possibly get away with." Even so, she wrote, the law "disgusted me, and it made me feel ashamed in a way I'd never been ashamed back in New York." Racial discrimination not only restricted the daily activities of blacks, Gibson learned, it also served as a constant reminder that many whites— including those who controlled the government—considered blacks inferior. But Gibson's sense of survival kept her from stirring up any trouble over the issue of racism. "I managed to conform to whatever the program was wherever I went," she wrote. "But I hated every minute of it."

Gibson knew that the South would never be her true home. Still, she decided to make the best of it while she was living there. She set out to make friends at Williston Industrial High School, signing up for the band, the choir, and the girls' basketball team. A good saxophone player, Gibson fit right in with the band, and her seemingly boundless athletic ability made her the star and captain of the basketball team. But when she showed up for rehearsals with the school choir, she ran into trouble. She was a strong singer, but her voice was so deep that the choir director put her in the tenor section with the boys. "The girls giggled so much about it," she wrote, "that I

got tired of it and quit." Indeed, many of her classmates seemed to view Gibson as something of an oddity.

Gibson began making friends at school when she joined a jazz group. Performing and relaxing in local nightclubs provided a welcome escape from life in the genteel Eaton household.

Gibson found it hard to get along with Wilmington's high school students, partly because she was older than most of them and a northerner as well. Her interests also set her apart from most of the girls at Williston Industrial High School. "I wasn't much for dressing up," Gibson noted. She preferred to spend her time practicing basketball or tennis, or playing baseball or football with the varsity boys' teams during their practices. "Look at her throwin' that ball just like a man," Gibson recalls the other girls saying. "They looked at me like I was a freak." Gibson was hurt by the cruelty of her classmates and confessed, "I showed off on the football field because throwing passes better than the varsity quarterback was a way . . . to show that there was something I was good at."

Fortunately, Gibson's interest in music brought her into contact with a small circle of friends who accepted her as she was. She had learned to play the saxophone in Harlem and was endowed with natural singing talent. Her musical ability earned her an invitation to join a jazz combo formed by a few senior boys in the school band. Gibson enjoyed playing weekend gigs with the group in local clubs. She liked having a little extra pocket money and relaxing with friends away from the confines of home and school. Soon, one of her new friendships turned into a romance. "The trumpet player had a big eye for me, and I liked him, too," she wrote. They started dating.

As she made friends, Gibson began to feel more comfortable in Wilmington. Her exuberance resurfaced, occasionally showing itself as rebelliousness. For the most part, Gibson was able to keep her mischievousness in check, but sometimes she could not resist temptation. One night, for instance, the Eatons went out with Dr. Eaton's mother, leaving Gibson at home doing homework. While Gibson studied, she kept looking at the elder Mrs. Eaton's car parked in the driveway. "How easy it would be to take off for a little joyride and come back before the doctor came home," she thought. She did not have a driver's license, but she had learned how to drive from Sugar Ray Robinson. After struggling briefly with her conscience, Gibson went downstairs, found the keys, and took off in the car. She picked up her boyfriend, went for a spin, and beat the Eatons home to park the car where she had found it.

If someone who knew the doctor had not seen her driving around town, Gibson would doubtless have gotten away with her stunt. But Dr. Eaton found out about the adventure the following morning. "I didn't see any point in pagelying to him," Gibson wrote. She confessed everything and apologized profusely to the furious doctor, who responded only with silence. Gibson felt sure that she was going to be sent back to New York. But, after allowing her some time to worry about her future, Dr. Eaton decided to permit her that one mistake. From that day on, Gibson wrote, she "tried to make sure he would never be sorry he had given me another chance."

Gibson's efforts paid off. She worked hard in school and by the end of her sophomore year ranked among the better students in her class. She put in even more time on the Eatons' backyard tennis court developing her athletic skill under the watchful eye of Dr. Eaton. There, she played against blacks from miles around, who flocked to Wilmington to use one of the only courts in the area open to blacks. Many white players who disagreed with the segregation laws also showed up to play. Gibson's competitors were almost always men, but her ever-improving tennis game proved too powerful for most of them. Dr. Eaton, Gibson recalled, "loved to see me beat the men he matched me against." She enjoyed it herself.

During the summers Gibson was free of academic concerns and could concentrate entirely on her tennis. At the end of the school year, she left Wilmington for the Lynchburg, Virginia, home of Dr. Johnson, her other benefactor, and his family. She spent the month of June practicing on the Johnsons' tennis court, often using the Tom Stowe Stroke

Developer. This machine automatically shoots tennis balls at a player across the net, who tries to return them as if to another player. Unlike human opponents, the machine never tires, so it provided Gibson with the kind of challenge she needed to build stamina and refine her strokes.

When July rolled around, Gibson started her tour of the ATA summer circuit. "Our traveling arrangements were far from luxurious," she noted. Crammed into a big Buick with Dr. Johnson, four or five other ATA players, and their luggage, she traveled as far north as New York, as far west as Missouri, and as far south as Florida. The tour was punctuated with rainstorms, bouts of blazing heat, flat tires, and stays in run-down motels. But Gibson loved to compete, and everything else faded to insignificance beside the thrill of tournament play.

When Gibson started playing the ATA circuit, it consisted of a series of weekly tournaments that ran through July and August. At each tournament, the country's finest black tennis players—generally the same players from week to week—met to test their skills against each other. The tour culminated in the ATA National Championships, held at the end of the summer. Gibson competed in the women's singles events and in mixed doubles

play with Dr. Johnson as her partner. In 1947 the ATA circuit consisted of nine tournaments. Gibson and Johnson took the mixed doubles title at eight of them, and on her own Gibson

A tennis student demonstrates the Tom Stowe Stroke Developer. The machine helped Gibson refine her stroking form and increase her stamina.

won all nine women's singles titles, including her first ATA National Championship.

That victory was the young player's first to be covered in the press, with "three or four lines of type at the bottom of the page in the *New York Times*," according to Gibson. It also marked the start of what would become a winning streak of 10 straight ATA National Championships. "For whatever it was worth," she wrote, "I was the best woman player in Negro tennis." Gibson hoped that her reign over the women's division of the ATA might lead to even bigger things. She dreamed of someday competing in the world's major tournaments, which were still off limits to blacks.

Gibson worked hard on both her studies and her tennis during her junior year of high school. In the summer of 1948, she repeated her success of the previous year, dominating every tournament she entered and winning her second consecutive national championship. Shortly after her victory, Dr. Eaton asked Gibson a simple question that opened a new chapter of her career. Referring to the most prestigious tennis tournament held in the United States—one that was closed to blacks—he asked, "Althea, how would you like to play at Forest Hills?"

Dr. Eaton knew Gibson would, as she put it, "give my right arm to play against the white girls." But to Gibson, the racial barrier in tennis seemed too great to be overcome, and she had always assumed the idea would never be anything more than a fantasy. She responded to the doctor's query with a flip "Who you kidding?" Dr. Eaton was not surprised by Gibson's answer, but instead of letting the issue drop he announced, "It could happen. People are working on it." Those people were ATA officials who believed Gibson was "the key they had been looking for to open the door" for blacks who wanted to compete in USLTA events. Gibson told the doctor, "I'm ready any time they are."

The ATA's efforts on behalf of Gibson soon yielded results. During Gibson's senior year of high school, white tennis officials notified the ATA that Gibson's entry to the Eastern Indoor Championships would be accepted. Indoor competition was considered less rigorous than outdoor play, but entry by a black player into any "white" tennis tournament represented an enormous step forward for blacks in tennis. Another black player, Dr. Reginald Weir, had competed against whites in indoor play two years earlier, but had made a poor showing and had not been invited to compete in later USLTA events. Gibson would now have a chance to prove herself against white tournament players.

The Eastern Indoor Championships were held in the 143rd Street armory in Harlem. Gibson felt good, she wrote, about playing "right in my own back yard," on courts where

she had played many times before. She was ranked last of the 32 women entered in the tournament, but she played well, winning her first 2 matches to advance to the quarterfinal. There she faced Betty Rosenquest, who knocked her out in 2 sets, 8-6, 6-0. "I was reasonably

Gibson attended high school in Wilmington, North Carolina (pictured), obtaining her diploma in three years. During the summer months, she lived in Lynchburg, Virginia.

satisfied," Gibson wrote of her performance. "At least I hadn't been disgraced." The USLTA was also pleased with Gibson's showing and invited her to play in the National Indoor Championships the following week. Gibson's ATA sponsors were thrilled. "It was ex-

actly the kind of progress they had been hoping for," Gibson wrote. As for herself, "I felt that I was on my way, that I was getting my fair chance." Gibson again played well. She made it all the way to the quarterfinal before losing to Nancy Chaffee.

Encouraged by the experience of her first two USLTA appearances, Gibson began making plans for her future. Throughout the end of her senior year she continued practicing tennis and studying hard. She made inquiries at several black colleges to find out if she would be eligible for a scholarship. Florida A&M University, located in Tallahassee, Florida, offered her a full scholarship and invited her to move south that summer to play tennis. In June 1949, Gibson graduated from high school, "tenth in my class if you please." She left Wilmington for Tallahassee two days later, eager to start life on her own again.

Gibson's consistently strong performance in ATA tournaments, plus the persistence of her supporters, eventually won her the chance to compete at indoor USLTA events.

Chapter Four

"All I Had Ever Asked for"

IN THE SUMMER of 1949, Althea Gibson won every ATA tournament she entered, including her third national championship. But despite her flawless ATA record and her respectable showing in indoor USLTA events earlier in the year, she was denied the chance to participate in outdoor USLTA play that summer. Unlike indoor tournaments, which were generally held in large public venues, outdoor events were conducted at private country clubs that did not permit blacks to play on their courts. Gibson began to understand that she needed more than talent to break into the

Driven by a personal goal—to prove herself as a world-class tennis player—Gibson unwittingly found herself in the forefront of the movement for racial equality.

USLTA. At the moment, though, she was more concerned about her imminent entry into college life. She left the fight for equal rights on the court in the hands of the ATA.

Florida A&M was one of the larger black colleges in operation at the time, but Gibson later wrote that it "wasn't exactly like the campus life I had always seen portrayed in the movies." The students were limited, either by school rules on campus or segregation laws off campus, in their choice of recreational activity. "Mostly we got along with a radio in our room, dances every now and then in the college gym, and movies in the auditorium," Gibson recalled. Students had to sign out and state their destination before leaving campus and had to return by a specified hour of the evening— 11:00 P.M. for seniors, 9:00 P.M. for freshmen. They were required to dress up for chapel services three times a week. "We thought it was ridiculous," Gibson wrote. Nonetheless, college afforded her more independence than she had enjoyed while living with the Eaton and Johnson families, and she was happy to be there.

Gibson's scholarship paid for her tuition, room, board, and books. Through the school's tennis coach, who had recommended her for the scholarship, she got a job assisting the director of women's physical education. The job provided her with spending money of $40 per month, "not that there was much I could do with the money," she noted. But Gibson did not really mind the lack of distractions, for she took a "serious view of college life." Besides, she had plenty of time to concentrate on developing her tennis game. Part of her plan was to continue competing in USLTA indoor tournaments.

In early 1950, during her freshman year at Florida A&M, Gibson traveled to New York to play in the Eastern Indoor Championships for the second time. She won that championship and entered the National Indoor Championships the next week. There, she advanced to the final before being soundly beaten, 6-2, 6-0, by Nancy Chaffee. Despite her defeat, Gibson wrote, she considered the tournament a "good experience for me, and even just getting to the finals was more than I had hoped for." Her performance also made her a celebrity at school. When she returned to Tallahassee, a crowd of students greeted her at the train station. The marching band turned out to play the school song, and the acting president of the university showed up to congratulate her in person. The campus was festooned with a big banner proclaiming: Welcome Home Althea!

Once again, however, Gibson's triumphs in indoor competition did not immediately

translate into invitations to that summer's outdoor USLTA tournaments. In Gibson's words,
"The USLTA acted as though I wasn't there."
Her frustration mirrored that experienced by
many black athletes of her era. Black boxers,
among them such champions as Joe Louis and
Sugar Ray Robinson, had long excelled in in-

A full athletic scholarship enabled Gibson to attend Florida A&M University in Tallahassee (above). The university was one of the largest schools for black students.

tegrated competition on equal terms with whites. But the other major professional and tournament sports played in the United States—baseball, football, tennis, golf, and basketball—remained segregated throughout most of the first half of the 20th century.

By the time Althea Gibson was in college,

the situation had begun to change. American society had been primed for a movement toward racial equality by World War II, which had ended in 1945. In that conflict, the United States had fought Japan for control of the Pacific region and had come to the aid of France and Britain in their fight against Nazi Germany and Fascist Italy. Although anti-Asian racism played a significant role in the struggle against Japan, Americans took pride in mobilizing to defeat the Nazis, who espoused an offensive philosophy of extreme racism. Americans had come to see themselves as protectors of the downtrodden. As a result, many whites felt more inclined to eradicate overt racial discrimination in the United States. And because so many black servicemen had fought and died for their country during the war, increasing numbers of whites had come to believe that blacks deserved equal opportunity at home.

In 1946 black baseball player Jackie Robinson made history by signing a contract to play alongside whites in the minor leagues. The following year he joined the Brooklyn Dodgers, becoming the first black to play major league baseball. The Dodgers won the 1947 National League pennant, and Robinson, who had batted .297 and led the league in stolen bases for the season, was voted Rookie of the

Year. Two years later, with a batting average of .342, he was voted Most Valuable Player of the National League. Even under conditions of intense pressure, Robinson's talent and drive led to success, opening the door for other black baseball players. Robinson also inspired efforts to break the racial barrier in other sports, such as tennis.

Segregation in tennis reflected not only conditions in the wider world but also the roots of the game itself. Lawn tennis originated in England in the late 19th century and came to the United States via Mary Ewing Outerbridge, a wealthy debutante from Staten Island, New York. The game quickly gained popularity among the upper classes of New York City, Philadelphia, Boston, and Newport, Rhode Island, and was played at exclusive clubs. In 1881 representatives of these clubs met to standardize the rules of play, and the United States National Lawn Tennis Association (which later became the USLTA) was born. The group regulated the evolution of the game, monitored tournaments held by affiliated country clubs, and sponsored the annual national championships. Men played in the first U.S. National Tennis Championships, held in Newport, in 1881; competition for a women's title was added in 1888. In 1915 the national championship tournament was mov-

ed to the West Side Tennis Club in Forest Hills, a prosperous neighborhood in the New York City borough of Queens. It had been played there ever since.

As a country club sport, tennis had remained the domain of wealthy whites. The construction in the 1940s of public tennis

Florida A&M's athletic program included the women's tennis team, shown a few years before Gibson's arrival. Gibson played on the team while attending college.

courts had widened participation in the sport somewhat, but private tennis clubs continued to control major tournament tennis in the United States. Very few of those involved in tennis at this level wanted to open the game to black players, so blacks were never invited to compete. The USLTA and its members masked their racist practices by rejecting "undesirable" tournament applications on the grounds that "not enough information" was submitted by the player. That is, when they did not wish to admit a player, they claimed that the player had not competed enough to demonstrate his or her qualifications to enter the tournament in question.

In 1950, however, as interest in Gibson mounted, the press began to criticize this practice. Gibson recalled, "The newspapers began to ask, if I wasn't given a chance to play, how could I ever prove myself?" But as the tournament season got under way in the spring of 1950, Gibson saw herself shut out of tournament after tournament. Summer arrived, bringing with it no better luck than spring had. Gibson knew that if the USLTA continued to bar her from its summer tournaments she would not be able to qualify to play at Forest Hills that September. The situation looked bleak, but Gibson would not give up the fight. Gibson's determination was founded on one simple belief: She felt that every person with talent and ambition deserved the chance to fulfill his or her potential. She had proven herself as a tennis player more conclusively than any white novice had ever been required to do. Now it was time for the USLTA to recognize her right to compete in its tournaments regardless of the color of her skin. Despite her campaign against the racist policies of the tennis establishment, Gibson wrote, "I have never regarded myself as a crusader. I try to do the best I can in every situation I find myself in, and naturally I'm always glad when something I do turns out to be helpful and important to all Negroes. . . . But I don't consciously beat the drums for any special cause, not even the cause of the Negro in the United States, because I feel that our best chance to advance is to prove ourselves as individuals." Gibson wanted simply to be accepted on her own merits and to be given a chance to play tennis against any worthy opponent.

Gibson knew that officials, rather than players, were the source of resistance to her inclusion in the USLTA. Indeed, most of the players were on her side, as she had discovered at the indoor events. She wrote that she was "made to feel right at home by the other girls" at the winter tournaments. "It wasn't just that they were polite; they were genuinely friendly, and believe me, like any Negro, I'm an expert at telling the difference." The majority of seasoned players on the USLTA circuit welcomed the fresh challenge presented by any talented new competitor. Gibson's way was blocked only by the bigotry and fear of those

who sat on the association's committee of directors.

Fortunately, a powerful member of the tennis community did not share the narrow view of the committee. That person was Alice Marble, whose dominance in women's tennis during the 1930s had earned her a place as one of the greatest players in the history of the

Jackie Robinson (shown), the first black to play major league baseball, not only opened the door for black baseball players but eased the way for the desegregation of other sports.

game. Marble, 1939 Wimbledon champion and four-time winner of the U.S. national title, had revolutionized women's tennis by introducing the hard-driving style that Gibson had admired eight years earlier at the Cosmopolitan Club. Disgusted with the racism displayed by others in her sport, Marble came to Gibson's aid. The most respected woman in tennis wrote a guest editorial in the July 1950 issue of American Lawn Tennis, the official publication of the USLTA. An eloquent argument against racial discrimination, the editorial read in part:

I think it's time we faced a few facts. If tennis is a game for ladies and gentlemen, it's also time we acted a little more like gentle people and less like sanctimonious hypocrites. If there is anything left in the name of sportsmanship, it's more than time to display what it means to us. If Althea Gibson represents a challenge to the present crop of women players, it's only fair that they should meet that challenge on the courts, where tennis is played. I know those girls, and I can't think of one who would refuse to meet Miss Gibson in competition. She might be soundly beaten for a while—but she has a much better chance on the courts than in the inner sanctum of the committee, where a different kind of game is played. I can't honestly say that I believe Miss Gibson to be a potential champion. . . . But if she is refused a chance to succeed or to fail, then there is an ineradicable mark against a game to which I have devoted most of my life, and I would be bitterly ashamed.

We can accept the evasions. . . . We can just "not think about it." Or we can face the issue squarely and honestly. . . . She is not being judged by the yardstick of ability but by the

Alice Marble (pictured) believed that Gibson should be allowed to compete in USLTA events. Marble referred to racist tennis officials as "sanctimonious hypocrites."

fact that her pigmentation is somewhat different.

If the field of sports has got to pave the way for all of civilization, let's do it. . . . The entrance of Negroes into national tennis is as in-

evitable as it has proven to be in baseball, in
football, or in boxing; there is no denying so
much talent. . . . Eventually the tennis world
will rise up en masse to protest the injustices
perpetrated by our policy makers. Eventually—why not now?

Alice Marble's bold statement first shocked,
then shamed the entire tennis establishment.

Gibson shakes hands with a defeated opponent at the National Clay Courts Championships in Chicago. Her success in outdoor USLTA tournaments silenced many of her critics.

Gibson's application to the New Jersey State Championships, submitted just as Marble's editorial appeared, was rejected. But then, "all of a sudden, the dam broke," Gibson wrote. She received an invitation to play in the Eastern Grass Court Championships, a major tournament, at the Orange Lawn Tennis Club in South Orange, New Jersey. She made it through the first round before losing in the second. The following week, Gibson was admitted to the National Clay Courts Championships in Chicago and advanced to the quarterfinal before being knocked out. Finally, "the big news came in the middle of August," according to Gibson. She was invited to play in the national championships at Forest Hills. "The USLTA announced it in a very matter-of-fact fashion," Gibson recalled, but "there was nothing matter of fact about it to me." Lawrence A. Baker, president of the USLTA, announced that Gibson had been "accepted on her ability." As Gibson remarked in her autobiography, "That was all I had ever asked."

The invitation to Forest Hills was a perfect gift for Gibson's 23rd birthday, which fell on August 25. But the young tennis player barely had time to celebrate, for she had only a few weeks to prepare for the tournament. She traveled to New York and settled in at the Harlem apartment of Rhoda Smith, one of her Cosmopolitan Club benefactors. Once the reality of the upcoming event sank in, Gibson wrote, "I began to worry about how I would react to playing in such an impressive place, a place I had never even seen." She called Sarah Palfrey Cooke, a USLTA player with connections at the West Side Tennis Club, and asked for her help. Cooke spoke to the club's president and arranged to take Gibson out to Queens for a private practice session and tour of the facilities. Gaining some familiarity with the venerable establishment helped calm Gibson's nerves.

On the day of her first match, Gibson packed her tennis clothes and equipment into a small bag and rode the subway out to Forest Hills with Rhoda Smith. At the club she registered for the tournament and found her way to the clubhouse locker room to change. In the locker room, she got her first glimpse of the world of big-time tennis. Reporters and photographers crowded around her, asking questions and snapping pictures. "The whole thing awed me," Gibson later remembered. "All this attention, all these people wanting to talk to me and get me to say things, patting me on the back and telling me that they knew I could do it. . . . I couldn't help wishing they would all go away and leave me alone." Little did she know that the press would not leave her alone again for years to come.

At 1:00 P.M. Gibson stepped onto Court 14 at the West Side Tennis Club and became a part of tennis history. Hordes of curious journalists milled around the edges of the court during the match, but Gibson easily defeated her opponent anyway. In 2 sets, with a score

of 6-2, 6-2, she eliminated Barbara Knapp of England and advanced to the second round of play. Afterward, in an interview with the press, Gibson "tried hard to be calm and poker-faced with the reporters," she wrote, "but I was pretty emotional deep down inside." Not only had she made it to Forest Hills, she was holding her own there.

Crowds of spectators—some supportive, some hostile, and others simply curious— watched Gibson's every move at the 1950 U.S. National Tennis Championships.

In the second round, held the next day, Gibson faced Louise Brough in one of the most dramatic matches ever witnessed. The newcomer battled tirelessly with the three-time Wimbledon champion and seemed on the verge of winning before a violent thunderstorm halted play. When the match resumed the following day, Brough quickly regained her footing and defeated Gibson. Nonetheless, Gibson's performance at the 1950 U.S. National Tennis Championships caused a sensation in the sports world. It launched her career in major tournament play and removed the barrier to black participation in top-level tennis. Althea Gibson had become a hero.

Sarah Palfrey Cooke (above), 1941 and 1945 U.S. national champion, showed Gibson around the West Side Tennis Club before Gibson's first appearance there.

Chapter Five

Goodwill Ambassador

AFTER HER APPEARANCE at Forest Hills, Althea Gibson returned to Tallahassee for her sophomore year of college. The year passed uneventfully until March 1951, when she was invited to play in the Good Neighbor Tournament in Miami. Her participation in a formerly all-white tournament in the Deep South marked another milestone for racial equality in tennis, but Gibson found the experience trying. "I felt as though I were on display, being studied through a microscope every minute," she later wrote. Fortunately, she soon had more auspicious things to think about.

For Gibson, the early 1950s were marked by frequent travel and numerous tournament appearances, but she failed to win any major titles or advance in the rankings.

Gibson's sponsors in the ATA, along with her newfound supporters in the USLTA, had arranged for her to travel to England that spring to become the first black ever to play in the All-England Tennis Championships. The contest, conducted since 1877 at the All-England Club in the London suburb of Wimbledon, was the sport's most prestigious tennis tournament. Wimbledon was, in a sense, the center of the tennis world. International tennis conventions, such as the standard dimensions of the court, the height of the net, the method of scoring, and the code of player etiquette, had been developed there.

Tennis players worldwide had come to regard competing at Wimbledon as a tremendous honor. Each year the tournament attracted the world's best players, each of them hoping to attain the ultimate tennis triumph: victory in the final of the All-England Championships, won on Centre Court before England's reigning monarch. Gibson had no realistic expectations of winning the tournament or even of becoming a semifinalist, which would enable her to play on Centre Court. But she was thrilled at the opportunity to travel abroad and participate in the world's premier tennis championship.

To help Gibson prepare for her trip, the USLTA arranged for her to go to the Detroit,

Boxing legend Joe Louis (in robe) offered Gibson the use of his hotel suite in Detroit while she trained for her first Wimbledon appearance. He also donated a round-trip airline ticket to London.

Michigan, suburb of Hamtramck for lessons with Jean Hoxie, one of the nation's most respected tennis instructors. To Gibson's great delight, she stepped off the plane to find herself a celebrity in Detroit's black community. Joe Louis, at that time the world heavyweight boxing champion and most famous of black athletes, had arranged for her to use his personal hotel suite during her stay. Knowing that Gibson would have to cover the expenses of her Wimbledon visit, Louis also presented her with a round-trip airplane ticket to London. To further ease Gibson's financial worries, a group of Detroit blacks held a benefit variety show that raised $770 for hotels, meals, and spending money for her trip.

"Unfortunately," Gibson remarked in *I Always Wanted to Be Somebody*, "a pocketful of money wasn't enough to win for me at Wimbledon." To her disappointment, she was decisively defeated in the contest's third round. Although she had broken Wimbledon's color barrier and advanced to the quarterfinal, Gibson knew she could have done better. The trip back home to America was a very long one indeed. Despite her setback, Gibson's game remained strong over the next few years. She won the ATA championship each summer from 1951 through 1955. She also continued to appear in numerous USLTA competitions and regularly advanced to the second or third round in most of them. Although she was a consistent and worthy player, Gibson failed to improve during this time. In 1952, competing for the first time in a nearly full schedule of USLTA tournaments, she was ranked as the ninth-best woman player in the United States. In 1953 she moved up to seventh place. But in 1954 she dropped down to the number 13 slot. Even more disappointing, that same year she was defeated in the very first round at Forest Hills. *Jet* magazine dubbed Gibson, The Biggest Disappointment in Tennis.

Gibson's name gradually disappeared from the headlines. Her glorious debut at Forest Hills had faded in the memories of sports fans, and her appearances in USLTA tournaments no longer caused a stir. Even the officials of the ATA seemed to lose interest in her as year after year she failed to become a champion. "Maybe I didn't get enough opportunities to play against topflight people," she conjectured in her autobiography.

It was during this difficult period that a new influence came into her life in the form of Harlem taxi driver and part-time tennis instructor Sydney Llewellyn. Llewellyn convinced the discouraged Gibson to stick with tennis and to try his innovative approach to the game. He took her game apart step-by-step, suggesting changes in her grip and stroke that increased the power of her shots. He drilled her on tennis strategies to improve

her court tactics. Gibson wrote that Llewellyn "kept me interested in the game" at a crisis point in her career.

Llewellyn's lessons and moral support meant a lot to Gibson, but her performance in important tournaments failed to improve. To observers, it seemed she lacked some key mental ingredient that would have allowed her to make the most of her physical ability. They

Maureen Connolly misses a backhand shot in a quarterfinal game against Gibson at the 1953 U.S. Nationals. Gibson lost the match, as she often did in the early 1950s.

theorized that a lack of confidence was causing her concentration to slip and allowing nervousness to take over at critical times during matches. Gibson also struggled to define herself off the tennis court, especially after her graduation from Florida A&M in June 1953. Through the efforts of her school's athletic director, she obtained a position as a physical education instructor at Lincoln

To support herself, Gibson took a job in the fall of 1953 as a physical education teacher at Lincoln University (above) in Jefferson City, Missouri.

University, a black school in Jefferson City, Missouri. Although she was grateful for the job, she felt frustrated with Missouri's strict racial segregation. There was virtually nothing to do off campus; not even the bowling alleys would admit blacks. The segregation both angered her and left her feeling humiliated, emotional states that undoubtedly resurfaced when she was participating as the only black in otherwise all-white tennis tournaments.

Gibson's dissatisfaction was further fueled by financial problems. Her salary at Lincoln was only $2,800 a year, barely enough for rent, car payments on a used Oldsmobile, and a few personal expenses. Her tennis career did little to ease her money worries. Because at that time even top tennis players were amateurs instead of professionals, they received no money (other than a small allowance for expenses) for competing in or even winning tournaments. By early 1955 the 27-year-old Gibson felt that she would never save enough money to help out her family or improve her standard of living unless she altered her goals.

Gibson's assessment of her future was influenced by a new relationship. She had begun dating a U.S. Army captain who headed Lincoln's Reserve Officers' Training Corps (ROTC) program. "Being in love," Gibson wrote in her memoirs, "and being loved by somebody, was something brand new to me." Although the romance eventually ended, it had a profound effect on Gibson, both personally and professionally. The captain urged her to pursue a career in the U.S. Army. He told Gibson that as a college graduate, she could enter the Women's Army Corps as an officer. She would receive free room and board, a good salary, and the opportunity for travel and advancement. After 20 years of service, she would be eligible for a pension. Given Gibson's precarious financial situation, an army career seemed quite attractive.

By the end of the school year in June 1955 Gibson had made up her mind. She submitted an admission application to the Women's Army Corps. Packing everything she owned into her Oldsmobile, she drove east to Harlem to inform her friends and family of her decision. Everyone, especially Sydney Llewellyn, begged her not to throw away all the years she had put into her tennis career. But Gibson told Llewellyn, "If I was any good I'd be the champ now. But I'm just not good enough. I'm probably never going to be."

Although her heart was not in it, Gibson continued to play tennis while she waited for word from the army. She was invited to play at Forest Hills in 1955, where she lost in the third round of what she thought was her farewell appearance. But something happened at Forest Hills that turned Gibson's career—and life—around. She was sitting at a table in the clubhouse when she was approached by Renville McMann, president of the West Side Tennis Club and a high-ranking official of the USLTA. He told her that the U.S. State Department was planning to send a team of four American tennis players—two men and two women—on a goodwill tour of Southeast Asia. "And," he added, "they specifically said they would like you to be on the team."

Gibson was pleased to travel with Karol Fageros (pictured) on a government-sponsored tennis tour of Southeast Asia. The tour sparked a lasting friendship between the two women.

In an instant, Gibson gave up her plans for an army career. "I told him the truth," she recalled of her response to McMann. "Not only would I consider it a great honor to make a trip like that but I was dying for something interesting to do." She knew one reason she had been chosen was that she was black. Among other things, the State Department wanted to show the world that the United States was moving toward racial equality. Yet she also knew that she would not have been selected if tennis authorities and the State Department did not believe she had the personal qualities to be an outstanding goodwill ambassador.

Gibson was excited by the chance to travel to such exotic countries as Thailand, Burma, Ceylon, India, Indonesia, and Malaysia. Her enthusiasm was further fueled when she learned that the other woman chosen for the trip was Karol Fageros. "I couldn't think of anybody I would rather spend a couple of months with," she wrote. She also liked Ham Richardson and Bob Perry, the two male players selected for the tour. All in all, the journey to Southeast Asia struck Gibson as a golden opportunity.

Even with such high hopes for the trip, Gibson's experiences far exceeded her expectations. One reason she enjoyed the tour so

"We had some great adventures on the tour," Gibson wrote of her trip through Asia. She saw exotic sights and won the All-Asian tennis championship in Rangoon, Burma, site of this pagoda.

When her tour through Southeast Asia concluded, Gibson traveled to Europe to prepare for an appearance in the 1956 All-England Tennis Championships at Wimbledon.

much, she reported, was that she was "the principal attraction of the group." As the American tennis stars traveled through the Far East, many Asians seemed to identify with Gibson because, like them, she had dark skin. "Because I was a Negro," she wrote in her autobiography, "the Asians were not only particularly interested in me, they also were especially proud of me. The kids looked at me, as I played, with awe and amazement."

While many of those who saw her play were awed by her athletic ability, Gibson, in turn, was dazzled by the Far East. She enjoyed many adventures during the tour, from experimenting with unfamiliar Oriental cuisines to visiting exotic cities. In Dacca, Pakistan, she saw city streets devoid of women because of *purdah*, the custom of keeping women out of public sight. Elsewhere she was entertained by belly dancers so nimble that she joked that their hips were "a modern engineering marvel." The friendships she formed with her fellow tennis players also made Gibson's tour memorable. "I'm an authority," she wrote in her autobiography, "on what it feels like to be the only Negro in all-white surroundings, and I can assure you that it can be very lonely." But the trip through Asia was different: Over the course of their two-month journey, she grew closer to her fellow tennis players and eventually no longer felt like an outsider. For the first time since she began to compete outside the black tennis circuit, she felt she was being judged for her tennis-playing ability, not her race.

Perhaps because of all the attention she was getting and the comradeship she enjoyed, Gibson's tennis started to improve dramatically. Her game grew more confident and more powerful from week to week. She won some local tournaments during the tour, then culminated the trip by winning the women's singles championship in the All-Asian Tennis Tournament in Rangoon, Burma. In January 1956 the tour made its final stop in Ceylon (now Sri Lanka). Gibson was sad to see the trip end, and she and Fageros cried when they parted. "I've never done anything more completely satisfying," Gibson later wrote, "or more rewarding, than that tour of Southeast Asia for the State Department." The tour had renewed Gibson's enthusiasm for tennis, and she was looking forward to the future with more excitement than she had felt in years. She would not give up on her game; instead, she resolved to do whatever was necessary to be the best. Her teammates returned to the United States, but she opted to remain in Europe. The Wimbledon championships were coming up that spring, and Gibson was determined to be ready.

Chapter Six

Centre Court

BEGINNING WITH HER victory in the women's singles championship in Burma, Althea Gibson put together a remarkable string of 16 victories in 18 international tournaments. She scored successes across Europe in such cities as Lyons and Cannes in France; Monte Carlo, Monaco; and Florence, Italy. The highlight of her extensive tour was the French Championships, a contest that ranked in importance just below Wimbledon and Forest Hills. On May 20, 1956, Gibson won the tournament by soundly defeating Angela Mortimer of England, 6-3, 11-9. She was not only

Gibson greets fans at a New York City ticker-tape parade after winning Wimbledon in 1957. For the next two years she would reign as the world's top female tennis player.

the first black to win a French national championship but the first black to win a major singles title anywhere in the world.

The strain of playing tournament after tournament finally caught up with Gibson when she reached England. She won four matches there, but each victory was a difficult struggle. As the Wimbledon contest drew near, British odds makers, impressed with Gibson's record, made her the 2-1 favorite to capture the tournament crown. But fate took a different course, and she fell to fellow American Shirley Fry in Wimbledon's quarterfinal, 4-6, 6-3, 6-4. In her autobiography, Gibson speculated that she had lost because she was "overtennissed." No other female player in the world had ever competed in so many consecutive tournaments. A second factor, however, may have been the real reason for her defeat.

After competing before so many friendly crowds across Asia and Europe, Gibson had once again been confronted with ugly racial tension as she fought for the Wimbledon crown. British reporter Scottie Hall remarked in the *London Sunday Graphic* that an "anti-Gibson atmosphere" had prevailed at Wimbledon. Hall charged that the crowd's "tight-lipped, cold" response to Gibson had contributed to her loss. Another journalist

Soon after completing her tour of Asia, Gibson won the women's singles title at the French Championships, one of the world's premier tennis events.

remarked that the tennis establishment was "riddled with snobbery" and agreed that the Wimbledon spectators had offered Gibson a chilly reception. Both writers applauded Gibson's attitude, which Hall termed "serenity and graciousness in unexpected, puzzling defeat."

Despite the results at Wimbledon, Gibson quickly regained much of the confidence that she had built up by winning 16 European tournaments. Although she lost again to Shirley Fry at the National Clay Courts Championships in Chicago, she won the Pennsylvania, Eastern States, and Pacific Southwest championships. At Forest Hills, she blasted her way to her first appearance in the final without losing a single set. But for the third time in three major championships, she lost to Shirley Fry, this time by a disappointing 6-3, 6-4.

Despite her inability to defeat Fry, 1956 was a remarkable year for Althea Gibson. Ranked 13th in 1954, she shot up to the number two spot. *World Tennis Magazine* recognized Gibson as a force to be reckoned with: "After four years of knocking at the door she suddenly consolidated her game, beginning one of the fastest climbs to the top in women's tennis." Gibson's goal for 1957 was to climb one more notch to become number one.

To further hone her game, Gibson accepted

an invitation from the Australian Lawn Tennis Association to join number-one-ranked Shirley Fry on a circuit of the major Australian tournaments. The trip was memorable for both women. Playing against some of the world's toughest competition, each captured two of the four major Australian championships, with Gibson winning the New South Wales and the South Australian contests and Fry taking the Victorian and the Australian nationals. The Australian press raved about Gibson's skill, terming her "a truly great athlete."

Between matches, as they explored Australia's cities and countryside, the women had ample opportunity to form a strong friendship. When Fry became involved in a whirlwind courtship with an American executive living in Sydney, Gibson became her confidante. At the end of the Australian tour Fry decided to remain in the country to marry her beau, but Gibson could not stay for the wedding: She had already signed on to go to Colombo, Ceylon, to defend her Asian championship.

Gibson retained her Asian title by beating England's Pat Ward, then returned home for a much-needed rest before traveling to Great Britain for the 1957 Wimbledon contest. To avoid making her previous mistake of going

to Wimbledon exhausted, Gibson entered only three of the warm-up tournaments. She arrived at Wimbledon "in top shape," she wrote.
"I wasn't tired and I wasn't worried." Her
first-round match was a grueling struggle with
a Hungarian named Suzy Kormoczy. Gibson
had to fight for every point, but she emerged
with a 6-4, 6-4 victory.

"Overtennissed" by the time she reached the 1956 Wimbledon tournament, Gibson lost to Shirley Fry in the quarterfinals, 4-6, 6-3, 6-4.

From there Gibson breezed to the semifinal, where she was up against 16-year-old sensation Christine Truman, the darling of British tennis fans. When Gibson took the court, she once again faced a hostile crowd. This time, however, as United Press International reported, "Gibson had command of her game right from the start." As she smashed winner after winner past the overmatched young Englishwoman, the spectators grew silent. Then the sheer brilliance of the black American's game won their admiration. When Gibson crushed her opponent, 6-1, 6-1, she walked off the court to resounding applause.

Althea Gibson had earned the opportunity to realize every tennis player's dream of walking out onto Wimbledon's Centre Court to play in the All-England Tennis Championships as the Queen of England looked on from the royal box. Gibson was extremely excited the night before the match. Fortunately, two old friends from the ATA had come to London to see the tournament. Their support helped keep Gibson relaxed and optimistic. The threesome enjoyed a leisurely dinner at a French restaurant before Gibson turned in early to get a good night's sleep.

Gibson woke up confident and well rested. She later recalled that the most difficult part of her warm-up preparations was practicing the curtsy she would perform when she was presented to the queen. Her curtsy went perfectly—and so did her tennis. Gibson's opponent in the final was Californian Darlene Hard, a Wimbledon semifinalist in 1955. Despite Hard's experience, it was Gibson who took command from the first serve, winning the first set, 6-3, in just 25 minutes. Then,

Shirley Fry (right) defeated Gibson repeatedly in 1956, but the two women became friends on a tour of Australian tournaments.

reported the *New York Times*, "The game grew faster as Miss Gibson's service jumped so alarmingly off the fast grass that Darlene nodded miserably as her errors mounted. It was all over in fifty minutes."

Shouting "At last! At last!" Gibson rushed to the net to shake hands with Darlene Hard. Then, as if in a dream, she watched while workers unrolled a red carpet that led from the royal box to the courtside trophy table. The woman who had been the "wildest tomboy in Harlem" stood at attention as the Queen of England approached her. Gibson curtsied, shook Queen Elizabeth's hand, and exchanged a few words with her. Then the British monarch handed her a gold salver (tray) inscribed with the names of Wimbledon's previous champions. Gibson wrote in her autobiography that at that moment, "I thought about something I had read in the book Helen Wills wrote about her career in tennis. 'My feelings,' she said, 'when the final Wimbledon match was mine, I cannot describe. This was the prize for all the games I have ever played since I was a little girl.' I knew exactly what she meant."

After posing for photographers, Gibson returned to the dressing room to find a huge stack of telegrams, including congratulations from boxer Sugar Ray Robinson, New York governor W. Averell Harriman, and President Dwight D. Eisenhower. That night, Gibson donned an evening gown to take on a new role—queen of the Wimbledon Ball. She gave a gracious speech, thanking everyone from

The first black to play at Wimbledon, Gibson defeated Darlene Hard (shown) on Centre Court to win the 1957 All-England championship.

Buddy Walker to Sydney Llewellyn to all her past opponents. Then, to the tune of "April Showers," Gibson danced with Wimbledon's male champion, Lew Hoad, while members of the Royal Family and the tennis establishment watched.

The celebration of Gibson's triumph continued when she returned to New York. A huge delegation that included reporters, city officials, and Gibson's mother met her plane at the airport. Then it was on to Harlem for an emotional homecoming. Gibson later commented that although meeting Queen Elizabeth was one of the high points of her life,

After Gibson won the women's singles final at Wimbledon, England's Queen Elizabeth presented her with a trophy in the form of a silver tray.

she was "telling the plain truth" when she said that it was even more moving "to have all those people come out of their tired old apartment houses up and down 143rd Street to tell me how glad they were that one of the neighbors' children had gone out into the world and done something big."

Crowning the glory for Gibson, the next day

New York City honored her with a ticker-tape parade up Broadway to the steps of City Hall, where Mayor Robert Wagner presented her with the medallion of the city. Then the mayor gave a gala luncheon in her honor at the posh Waldorf-Astoria Hotel. There was now no doubt—after years of hard work and disappointments, Althea Gibson had finally become "somebody."

Although she was proud of what she had accomplished, both for herself and for other blacks, Gibson was somewhat uncomfortable with her new status as an international symbol of black achievement. "What am I supposed to be, a special assistant to the secretary of state, or something?" Gibson wondered in her autobiography. "I tried to think of myself as just another person," she wrote. But she was constantly reminded that she was instead "a special sort of person—a Negro with a certain amount of international significance." For a woman as private as Gibson, her newfound status was "pleasant to think about but very hard to live with."

The bottom line for Gibson was tennis, not championing causes, an attitude that sometimes puzzled other blacks. She admired the work of civil rights leaders such as Martin Luther King, Jr., but she did not feel that she possessed the gifts of oratory or organization that would make her valuable to the civil rights movement. Although she was stung by occasional attacks in the black press, Gibson kept to her course. "I feel strongly," she wrote, "that I can do more good my way than I could by militant crusading. I want my success to speak for itself as an advertisement for my race."

Characteristically, after her Wimbledon triumph Gibson's thoughts quickly returned to her game. Picking up where she had left off, she easily won the National Clay Courts tournament in Chicago. Next she moved on to the Wightman Cup, the prestigious international competition between the United States and Great Britain, and she led the U.S. team to victory.

The summer tennis season culminated in the U.S. championship at Forest Hills. By chance, Gibson's first-round opponent was Karol Fageros, her close friend and companion from the Southeast Asian tour. Perhaps because she hated to see her friend lose, Gibson struggled before winning, 6-4, 6-4. After this match, however, she pulled out all the stops. Playing with supreme confidence, she defeated four more opponents without losing a single set. Now, only the final stood between Gibson and the number one spot in women's tennis.

She thought it somehow appropriate that her opponent in the final was Louise Brough. Seven years before, Brough —with the aid of

a thunderstorm—had defeated Gibson in her first Forest Hills appearance. This time, however, not even a hurricane could have held Gibson back. The prestigious Forest Hills crown was hers after an easy 6-3, 6-2 victory.

Gibson's proud parents look on as New York City mayor Robert Wagner presents her with the medallion of the city. Gibson's 1957 Wimbledon victory made her a hometown hero.

Gibson found winning the championship of her own country even more thrilling than her Wimbledon victory. Vice-president Richard Nixon presented her the trophy while the crowd showered her with applause that officials declared was the warmest and most sustained they had ever heard. There was absolutely no question now that Althea Gibson was the best female tennis player in the world. Writing of the experience in her autobiography, Gibson reported, "All I know is that nothing quite like it had ever happened to me before, and probably never will again."

Gibson played in a few more U.S. tournaments in 1957, then collected the Babe Didrikson Zaharias Trophy as the year's outstanding female athlete. Soon, however, Gibson's thoughts turned to rest and recreation. She arranged invitations to several winter tournaments in the Caribbean and South America. All of her expenses were paid by the promoters of the tournaments in which she played, and she concentrated on relaxing, seeing the sights, and enjoying her well-earned success. Refreshed by her trip, Gibson returned home and began training hard for her upcoming matches. The spring 1958 season opened on a sour note as she played poorly in the competition for the Wightman Cup, and the United States lost to Great Britain for the first time in 26 years. As the Wimbledon competition drew near, some observers thought she would have trouble defending her title. Gibson was determined to prove that last year's win had been no fluke. She got off to

Darlene Hard, Althea Gibson, Dorothy Head Knode, Louise Brough, and Margaret Osborne (left to right) made up the victorious 1957 U.S. Wightman Cup tennis team.

a shaky start at Wimbledon, barely surviving a difficult three-set quarterfinal match with Shirley Bloomer, the top-ranked British player. She then regained her confidence, blasting Ann Haydon, 6-2, 6-0, in a 31-minute

pagesemifinal. Gibson then went on to vanquish Angela Mortimer, 8-6, 6-2, for her second All-England championship. Once again, she felt on top of the world as she danced in the spotlight at the Wimbledon Ball.

Gibson remained in top form after her return to the United States and won several tournaments before moving on to Forest Hills.

Vice-president Richard Nixon presents Gibson with the winner's trophy at the 1957 U.S. National Tennis Championships. That victory was even sweeter to Gibson than her triumph at Wimbledon.

She had little difficulty in the U.S. Nationals until her final match with Darlene Hard, the Californian she had defeated for her first Wimbledon crown. Gibson made several mistakes and lost the first set, 3-6. Then, in a lightning-quick turnaround, she began playing some of the best tennis of her life, crushing Hard, 6-1, 6-2 to defend her U.S. championship.

Gibson's victory solidified her ranking as the best female tennis player in the world. The question among tennis observers was no longer, will Gibson make it? but rather, how long can she stay on top? But Althea Gibson, a woman whose life had been marked by many sudden changes of fortune, had been weighing her future for months. On September 7, 1958, moments after she stepped off the court where she had triumphed over Darlene Hard, she made an announcement that shocked the world of tennis.

Chapter Seven

The Professional

REPORTERS SWARMED AROUND Althea Gibson as she prepared to leave the West Side Tennis Club, where she had just won her second consecutive U.S. National Tennis Championship. Expecting to record the usual remarks of a player flushed with victory, they were not prepared for Gibson's opening bombshell: "I wish to announce my retirement from the ranks of amateur tennis players. I am tentatively setting a period of retirement at one year."

After retiring from amateur tennis in 1958, Gibson tried her hand at several moneymaking ventures, including a tour with Karol Fageros (right) as the opening act for the Harlem Globetrotters.

The astonished reporters besieged her with questions: When had she made her decision? What would she do next? And above all, why would an athlete who had finally reached the top after 15 years of hard work possibly want to quit? In Gibson's mind, the answer to the last question was simple: money. Tennis had made Gibson famous, but it certainly had not made her rich. She told the *London Daily Mail* in 1956 that she was then "as poor as when I was picked off the back streets of Harlem and given the chance to work myself up to stardom. . . . I am much richer in knowledge and experience. But I have no money."

Althea Gibson's precarious financial situation may seem strange today, when most top tennis players are professionals who receive large payments for appearing in competitions. But in the 1950s most exhibition players were amateurs who received nothing except small payments that barely covered their expenses. Professional tennis, in which various sporting-goods companies or other corporations sponsored tournaments, had enjoyed a brief heyday in the late 1930s and early 1940s. But it was limited to men and the prizes were less than generous, and the endeavor withered away after World War II. By the 1950s only a small group of players with salaries paid by sponsoring businesses were considered professionals. These athletes played exhibition matches and made public appearances for promotional purposes. The majority of players, though, chose to remain amateurs and compete on the traditional tournament circuit. They often accepted under-the-table payments for their appearances, but it would be another 10 years before tournaments would start awarding official cash prizes to winners, ushering in the era of high-stakes professional tennis.

Because competitive tennis was so financially unrewarding, Gibson found herself in an odd position: She was at the pinnacle of her career, yet she was virtually penniless. Gibson was leading a hand-to-mouth existence even though she had achieved every goal she had set for herself in amateur tennis. She was the number one female player in the world, champion of the United States, Great Britain, France, Asia, Mexico, and India. She had been honored by royalty and presidents, and her name had appeared in newspaper headlines in dozens of countries. But in 1958 the 31-year-old Gibson lived in a small New York City apartment partially filled with furniture she had found on the streets of the city. She had no bank accounts, no investments, no regular income. One of the reasons that she had traveled so much over the last few years was that her living expenses were paid only when she

was competing in tournaments.

Gibson's decision to announce her retirement after her second Forest Hills victory arose from her feeling that she deserved to reap some financial rewards from her years of hard work. She wanted to buy some nice things for herself and help her still impoverished parents escape the slums of Harlem. Once she determined that amateur tennis was a dead end financially, she faced another difficult issue: How could she best capitalize on her name and talents?

Other players in her position often solved this problem by signing on as teaching professionals at tennis clubs. But because Gibson was black she could not take this route. The wealthy whites who made up the memberships of tennis clubs, most of whom had only reluctantly accepted Gibson as a tournament player, were not eager to hire a black professional to teach them the game. Since this avenue was closed to her, Gibson began to consider moving away from sports entirely. She hoped that her fame might help her pursue another longtime dream: singing.

A talented vocalist with a rich voice, Gibson attempted to launch a singing career. She released an album and made two television appearances but went no farther in the music industry.

Gibson had always had a strong, full voice, and in 1943 she had captured second prize in a talent competition at Harlem's famed Apollo Theater. Throughout her athletic career she had often been asked to sing at tennis banquets and other occasions, including the Wimbledon balls. In 1956 she had made several test recordings at a studio in London, and in 1957, anticipating her retirement from tennis, she had hired a vocal coach to polish her technique. Since then, she had been taking lessons three times a week.

Gibson's career as a singer got off to a promising start. Her performance at a 1958 testimonial dinner led to an album contract with Dot Records. The name of the lead song, which also served as the title of her second autobiography, was "So Much to Live For," a phrase Gibson felt summed up her life. Just prior to the album's release she was invited to sing on "The Ed Sullivan Show," the most popular television variety program of the 1950s. Gibson was a hit, and she made a second appearance on the show later in 1958. Although her fame opened doors for her in the music industry, it could not ensure her success. The sales of her album, *Althea Gibson Sings*, were extremely poor. She received few offers for appearances on television shows or in nightclubs. It began to look as if singing would be no more lucrative than tennis.

Undaunted, Gibson next pursued an acting career. She obtained a significant role in *The Horse Soldiers*, a Western by acclaimed director John Ford. The film starred two of Hollywood's most famous actors, John Wayne and William Holden. Appearing in the movie was a thrill for Gibson, who had spent a good portion of her childhood in movie theaters. She worked very hard on the film, and when it appeared in 1959 her performance elicited generally good reviews. Yet there were few movie roles for blacks during this period, and Gibson received no further offers.

Fortunately for Gibson an unexpected opportunity greatly diminished her singing and acting disappointments. The offer came from Abe Saperstein, the owner of the Harlem Globetrotters. An all-black basketball team formed in 1930, the Globetrotters toured the world playing exhibition games that blended comedy with serious basketball. By the 1950s they were a much-loved American institution, playing to capacity audiences wherever they traveled.

In order to round out the Globetrotters' performances and attract more fans, Saperstein complemented their appearances with some other form of entertainment. In 1959 he decided that a tennis exhibition might be popular,

and he offered Gibson a contract. He asked her if she would open each Globetrotter game by playing a round of tennis, in which she would be matched against either a local star or another professional traveling with the show. Gibson enthusiastically accepted Saperstein's offer. She formed a corporation with her

Gibson (left) appeared with William Holden (center) and John Wayne (far right) in The Horse Soldiers. *Her acting career, however, failed to take off.*

coach, Sydney Llewellyn, and her lawyer to handle the business end of the deal. Althea Gibson Enterprises received a flat fee for each performance, out of which came travel expenses, the salaries of a road manager who set up and took down the court before each game, and the salary of the second player.

Gibson's tennis exhibitions proved extremely popular, for two reasons. First, even fans who had come just to see the Globetrotters were quickly awed by Gibson's power and grace on the tennis court. The second factor was Gibson's shrewd choice of a touring partner: Karol Fageros, who had accompanied Gibson on her trip through Asia. Fageros, known by some tennis fans as the Golden Goddess because of her powerful game and fair-haired beauty, was a worthy opponent for the formidable Gibson. Together they often played brilliant matches that held their audiences spellbound.

Gibson discovered that the life of a roving performer had its good and bad sides. Although she had toured extensively during her amateur tennis days, she had never before kept to a schedule as hectic as the Globetrotters'. Moving to new cities on an almost daily basis was grueling, and Gibson often felt tense and lonely. But when the tour ended in New York in July 1960, Gibson felt a sense of real satisfaction. She was back on the tennis courts and was finally earning a decent living.

For the first time in her life, Althea Gibson had some money in the bank. She was able to move to a nice apartment. And even more important to her, she placed a down payment on a 10-room house in the suburbs, so that she could finally move her parents and the rest of her family out of Harlem. Gibson proudly wrote, "When they open their front door they can see the green of grass and the blue of sky, and there is no smell of refuse, no prostrating heat, no fear of violence."

Now that the present was secure, Gibson turned her attention to the future. Because the crowds had responded so enthusiastically to the tennis matches that preceded Globetrotter games, Abe Saperstein asked Gibson to accompany the team on an overseas tour. But she and her advisers were examining another option. Although Althea Gibson Enterprises had made an excellent profit on the Globetrotters tour, the basketball team had made appreciably more. If Althea Gibson Enterprises had organized the tour, they reasoned, its profits would have been so great that the figures, in Gibson's words, "made us just a little giddy with greed." She turned down the offer from the Globetrotters and decided to organize her own basketball-tennis tour.

The decision turned out to be a terrible

mistake. Gibson described the key error: "I'm
sad to say that we left out of these calculations
an intangible but critical factor, namely the
prodigious reputation of the Globetrotters
themselves." In other words, their logic was
as faulty as the assumption that, for example,
baseball fans would be just as eager to see a
team they had never heard of as they would

Gibson clowns for the camera with tennis partner Karol Fageros and Harlem Globetrotters owner Abe Saperstein. Her stint with the Globetrotters was highly successful.

be to watch the New York Yankees or the Los Angeles Dodgers.

Instead of performing before full arenas, as the Globetrotters had, Althea Gibson's sports exhibitions were playing to empty seats in town after town. The losses mounted steeply. When the tour was canceled after three months, Gibson was, in her words, "ruined

financially." Not only were her bank accounts wiped out, but she was saddled with a huge debt. Compounding the loss was the behavior of her partners, who Gibson believed abandoned her in the crisis and even stole some of the

Gibson traveled extensively during her tenure with the Globetrotters, playing before capacity audiences in gyms and auditoriums across the country.

assets of her failing corporation.

The failure of Althea Gibson Enterprises was the low point of her life. Yet once again, an unexpected offer became a lifeline that gave Gibson an opportunity to support herself and

As a community relations representative for the Ward Baking Company, Gibson endorsed its products in advertisements and made many public appearances.

to begin to pay off her debts. The invitation came from the Ward Baking Company, a large corporation that produced an array of baked goods, including Tip Top Bread. Out of the blue, Gibson was contacted by Ward and offered a job in their community relations department. For a salary of $25,000 a year—a lot of money at that time—Gibson would serve as Ward's spokeswoman. She would travel from city to city, making appearances on radio and television shows, at civic functions, school assemblies, and charity affairs.

Gibson gave talks on her career and answered questions about tennis. She proved to be a very inspirational and popular speaker, and Ward rehired her for a second year. But despite the bright, enthusiastic manner she adopted for her public relations work, Gibson was suffering privately. She seldom ventured from her hotel rooms, preferring to sit by herself and brood. She wrote, "Everything worth living for, it seemed to me then, existed in the past; money, glory, prestige, popularity and publicity, love and friendship, all glowed with the yellow luster of unpolished trophies." She had always been a person driven by a dream, a goal. Now that she had none, she sank into depression.

After two years of what she called "hibernation," Gibson's powerful determination and

drive began to reassert itself. Once again, she began to long for the thrills of athletic competition. She had no intention of returning to tennis, because the sport still held no prospect of providing her with an income to support herself and her family. Instead, she became

Frustrated with life as a former champion, Gibson yearned to compete again. She took up golf in the hope of becoming a top tournament player.

increasingly interested in another athletic pursuit.

Back in the mid-1950s, Gibson had first tried her hand at golf. She had enjoyed the game and played it occasionally since then, and during the second year of her affiliation with

Ward Baking, she began to play more frequently in order to occupy her time in strange cities. Her superior athletic ability and great strength gave her a tremendous advantage over even experienced players. Golf professionals who saw her play raved about her potential. "Gibson has everything," remarked one awed pro. "The swing, the hands, the touch, the temperament. . . . She hasn't played much, but give her a year of work and she could be the greatest."

As Gibson considered the idea of becoming a professional golfer, she realized that she would face major obstacles. The first was her age. Although she was only 33 years old when she began to think about joining the pro circuit, she knew that the vast majority of professional golfers had learned the sport as children. Even with her great natural ability, she would have to spend years making up for lost time. She might be close to 40 years old by the time she was ready to challenge the top golfers.

Another serious obstacle was an old enemy that Gibson had faced in tennis—racial prejudice. Almost all professional golf tournaments were conducted at private country clubs that did not accept blacks as members and almost never as guests. Black men had made small inroads into the game, but in 1962 no black had ever played in a Ladies Professional Golf Association (LPGA) tournament. Unintimidated, Gibson once more decided to defy tradition. She hoped that her ability would eventually win her the opportunity to compete, just as it had in tennis. Gibson also worried about supporting herself while she honed her golf game, but her concerns were alleviated by a generous offer from the Ward Baking Company. Even though Ward had hired her because of her reputation as a tennis player, they agreed to keep her on while she devoted her energies to golf. They also promised to rearrange her schedule of promotional engagements to accommodate her golf lessons and tournament appearances.

In 1962 and 1963, Gibson devoted herself to the long, tedious, and lonely task of perfecting her golf game. She found the sport much harder to learn than tennis. The main reason was that golf required great patience and self-discipline but provided no outlet for the nervous energy and frustration that built up as she worked to master the game. In tennis, she could channel her emotions into running faster and smashing a tennis ball harder. On the golf course, all she could do was grit her teeth.

Fortunately, Gibson found great emotional support in a man named Will Darben. Darben was the brother of Rosemary Darben, one of her best friends. Years before, during her slump in the early 1950s, Gibson had often stayed at the Darben family's New Jersey home for long periods of time, and she and Will had formed a strong friendship. He had fallen in love with her and proposed marriage in 1953. But Gibson was devoting all of her emotional energy to her tennis at the time. She thought of Will Darben more as a friend than a husband, and she turned him down. Darben and Gibson had kept in touch over the years, and he was especially supportive during the difficult times she faced in 1961 and 1962. Gibson's affection eventually turned into stronger feelings of love. At the end of 1963 she found herself close to accepting his renewed marriage proposals.

Gibson's professional life was also taking shape during this period. She was beginning to feel that her golf game had achieved what she called a "groove." She decided 1964 would be the year she would break yet another color barrier. She would enter golf tournaments sponsored by the LPGA.

Chapter Eight

"So Much to Live For"

ALTHEA GIBSON REGARDED 1964, in her words, "not so much as a year [but] as a battlefield." On that battlefield, she planned to launch an offensive to become a top professional golfer. The first phase of her strategy would be a full frontal assault on the all-white Ladies Professional Golf Association (LPGA), the governing body of the women's professional golf tour. Gibson's challenge in attempting to storm the LPGA would be quite different from the one she had faced when breaking into the USLTA, for the two associations were different in their organization and mode of operation.

Even though she did not play the game seriously until she was in her thirties, Gibson enjoyed an admirable golf career that spanned the years 1964 through 1970.

The LPGA's membership consisted solely of professional women golfers. Its director was responsible only to this membership, not to a board of private club officers. Thus, individual golfers had much more clout in the LPGA than did tennis players in the USLTA. The LPGA took a more active role than its tennis counterpart in organizing the annual circuit of golf tournaments across the country, working with local sponsors in each city as well as with the members of the golf clubs at which tournaments were held.

Most of the 25 to 35 tournaments on the LPGA tour were "open," meaning that any golfer could enter by paying a fee of $50 to $100. The golf club at which the tournament was being held had the power to veto an individual entry for any reason. LPGA members who held player's cards were exempt from entry fees and largely protected from being vetoed by club management. Membership could also help a golfer gain entrance to the small number of tournaments that were "invitational," meaning they were open only to players invited by the sponsoring golf club. Although these clubs weren't required to invite every golfer who was a member of the LPGA, the association could remove from its tournament roster any country club that regularly refused to invite a significant number of its members.

The considerable power wielded by the LPGA on behalf of its members was why Gibson was so determined to win her player's card—proof of membership in the LPGA. She had learned from her experience in tennis that racist whites might try to block her way no matter how well she played. She knew that if she were to pursue her goal of becoming a professional golfer on her own, it might take years to break down the racial barrier at country clubs. If she could gain the support of the LPGA, however, she felt sure that she would win acceptance much more quickly.

The actual requirements for obtaining full membership in the LPGA were simple: A golfer had to finish in the top 80 percent of those entered in 3 out of 4 consecutive tournaments. Gibson felt confident about her ability to prove herself on the golf course. And since the LPGA was an association of athletes rather than of country clubs and wealthy patrons, she hoped that her performance would count for more than her race among its membership, as it eventually had in the USLTA.

The support of other tennis players had been a key factor in Gibson's entrance into the USLTA, and her first experiences in golf competition had included a warm welcome from

most of the other golfers. At the few tournaments in which Gibson played in 1963 she
had not done very well, compiling a scoring
average of 84.5 strokes for 18 holes in tournaments where the better players averaged no

Gibson clowns for the camera with tennis partner Karol Fageros and Harlem Globetrotters owner Abe Saperstein. Her stint with the Globetrotters was highly successful.

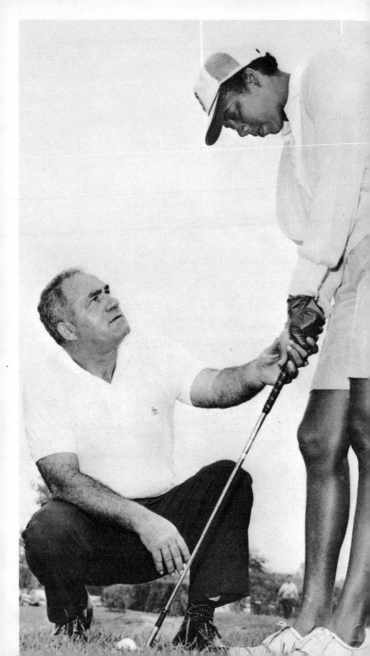

more than 74 strokes. But the other competitors had been friendly and encouraging, just as the white tennis players had been during her first USLTA appearances so many years before.

Now, in 1964, Gibson set out to win her player's card. She began the year slowly, doing poorly in several springtime tournaments. But as the weather warmed toward summer, Gibson's game heated up, too. Her scoring average dropped 7 strokes, from 84 to 77, a remarkable improvement. She finished in the top 80 percent in 2 tournaments in a row, and needed to do as well in only 1 more to earn the prized player's card.

The next tournament Gibson entered was held at a country club that, while it would allow her to play on its course, refused her entry to the clubhouse. She had nowhere to change her clothes, take a shower, or eat lunch. Concentrating on achieving her goal, Gibson coolly dismissed the club's rule as "silliness" and "ac-

Determined to become a respected professional player, Gibson devoted most of her waking hours to her golf game. Here, Jerry Volpe gives her some advice.

cepted their treatment with half-amused resignation." It was not that she took the situation lightly. But she knew that the club would be more than paid back with unfavorable coverage in the press. The issue of civil rights and the growing movement for racial equality had begun making headlines across the country, and instances of discrimination such as that experienced by Gibson always got into the newspapers. Gibson believed that bad publicity would eventually produce more social change than she could by causing a fuss at the club.

Gibson took her own sweet revenge by playing one of her best tournaments so far. She finished ahead of nearly half the other players, and finally won the right to a player's card. As she had hoped, the LPGA willingly granted her membership. Times had indeed changed in the past dozen years.

As a member of the LPGA, Gibson had the official support of the association and its dynamic director, Leonard Wirtz. Wirtz devoted himself wholeheartedly to the LPGA and to each of the group's members. He was famed for his unflagging zeal for promoting women's golf and for his unique combination of determination and charm. In him Gibson had a powerful and persuasive ally. Whenever she was refused entrance to a country club's clubhouse, Wirtz vigorously argued against the ban. If his arguments went unheeded, he threatened more drastic action. On at least three occasions, Wirtz moved tournaments to different clubs or new cities in response to persistent discrimination against Gibson.

The support of Wirtz and the legitimacy conferred by membership in the LPGA allowed Gibson to shift her attention from gaining access to tournaments to her performance in them. Unfortunately, she found that reaching the top of the game was much more difficult than getting the chance to play it. Somehow, she did not seem to be able to muster the steadiness, polish, and concentration that golf required. At the 1964 Thunderbird Open in Phoenix, Arizona, for instance, Gibson's performance was typically uneven. She shot a 69, her best score ever, in the first round, taking the lead. But the next day, her concentration wavered and she miscalculated her score, which constitutes a serious breach in the rules of golf. When she turned in an incorrect scorecard she was disqualified from the tournament.

Gibson continued to struggle with her golf career throughout the 1964 season, making gradual improvements and winning a few tournaments. She won $561.50 in prize money, compared with the $29,800 claimed by Mickey

Wright, the leading money winner in women's golf that year. Gibson was proud of having finally made money in athletic competition and looked forward to advancing in 1965.

Before the 1965 season began, Gibson faced another financial crisis. Ever since golf had turned into a full-time job, it had been difficult for her to fit promotional appearances for the Ward Baking Company into her schedule. Gibson had so little time available for this work that Ward reluctantly decided not to renew her contract. Gibson tried to find another sponsor who would provide her with the $750 to $1,000 a month she needed to stay on the professional golf tour. When she failed to locate a new source of income, she took out a bank loan. With money in the bank, Gibson continued to pursue her golf career. She made some progress, lowering her scoring average slightly and boosting her winnings to $1,595.00. It fell far short of the amount of her loan, but it was enough to convince the bank to extend her loan for another year.

Gibson's golf game peaked in 1967. By the time she appeared in the 1969 U.S. Women's Open (pictured), she was struggling to maintain a consistent level of play.

Late in 1965, with her golf career well under way, Gibson decided to marry Will Darben. They were wed in a ceremony in Las Vegas, Nevada. Her marriage provided Gibson with a new measure of financial and emotional security. Darben's job prevented him from traveling with her on the golf tour, but Gibson now had a home to return to after the often frustrating months and weeks on the circuit. Married life also seemed to boost Gibson's confidence in 1966. She lowered her scoring average to 74 and more than doubled her earnings, to $3,221.50. The highlight of her year was scoring a 68 to break the course record at the Pleasant Valley Country Club in Sutton, Massachusetts.

But 1967 turned out to be the last year of significant improvement in Gibson's golf game. Despite all her hard work over the next three years, she was unable to achieve the consistently impressive performance that had taken her to the top of the tennis world. On occasion she would play an excellent round, only to follow it with a weak showing. From 1967 through 1970 she never finished the season among the top 10 players, either in scoring average or in money earned. By the end of 1970, her seventh year on the professional golf tour, Gibson realized that her golf earnings were unlikely to ever equal her expenses.

Although she had carefully controlled her spending, she was thousands of dollars in debt. Gibson decided it was time to move on again.

Looking back, Gibson felt proud of some of her accomplishments as a golfer. Once again, she had helped pave the way for other black athletes in a sport that had long been open to only whites. She had overcome great odds to become proficient in the sport while in her thirties. Despite these obstacles, she had established herself as a capable middle-level competitor. But now it seemed to her that her greatest opportunity lay in her original field: tennis.

Since 1958, when Gibson retired from competitive tennis, a tremendous change in racial attitudes had taken place in America. By 1971 few private clubs hesitated to hire black tennis professionals. Gibson found a job teaching tennis in New Jersey. Two years later, she had saved enough money to invest in an indoor club there. As a professional, Gibson spent a lot of time on the courts. Her confidence in her game revived, and she began to consider making a comeback in competitive tennis. Part of the appeal of returning to tennis was that it was now possible to make a living in the game. Beginning in 1968, all major tournaments paid prize money. As a result, virtually all of the best professional players earned a very good

In 1971, Gibson considered a return to tournament tennis, which had begun offering cash prizes. Top competitors such as Martina Navratilova (left) and Steffi Graf (above) have since become wealthy playing the game.

Gibson's drive to earn recognition in her sport paved the way for participation in tennis by such black players as Arthur Ashe (below) and Zina Garrison (right).

In recent years Gibson has enjoyed introducing children to tennis. She has become a role model for many young blacks with athletic ambition.

living from their sport.

Gibson thought that she could do well in professional tennis and made inquiries about returning to competition. But when she applied to play at the U.S. Open at Forest Hills, she was informed that she would have to play in a designated number of preliminary rounds in order to qualify. Gibson was shocked that as a former world champion she was still being asked to qualify. She did not want to risk losing against an unknown young player in a qualifying round. In her own words, "That turned me off, and I didn't pursue it any further." Gibson returned to teaching tennis but soon found her life fraught with disappointments. Her tennis club failed financially and shut down. Her marriage came to an end.

Gibson once again chose a new course for herself. She accepted an offer from the city of East Orange, New Jersey, to manage its Department of Recreation. East Orange, a poor city with a large black population, reminded Gibson of Harlem. She found great satisfaction in reaching out to the local children, just as Buddy Walker, the play-street supervisor who introduced her to tennis, had reached out to her. By giving them the opportunity to channel their energies and build confidence through sports, Gibson hoped to make a difference in their life. Her dedication made her a local celebrity and a hero to the children of East Orange. For many she became a source of inspiration, much as Sugar Ray Robinson had been to her so many years before.

Today, Gibson still teaches tennis professionally and plays frequently. After so many years in the spotlight she has settled into a quiet life, but her achievements remain as dazzling as ever. She occupies a permanent place in both the history of sports and the history of civil rights. As tennis writer Stan Hart put it, "You mention Althea Gibson, and you also think of Martin Luther King, Jr., and Jackie Robinson." Like Jackie Robinson, Gibson opened doors for blacks in her sport and showed how hard work and dedication can lead to outstanding achievement in any field. And like Dr. Martin Luther King, Jr., Althea Gibson, through her dignity, courage, and sheer talent, opened the world's eyes to the senselessness and injustice of racism.

FURTHER READING

Aaseng, Nathan. *Winning Women of Tennis.* Minneapolis: Lerner Publications, 1981.

Ashe, Arthur R., Jr. *A Hard Road to Glory: A History of the African-American Athlete 1619-1918.* New York: Warner Books, 1988.

_____.*A Hard Road to Glory: A History of the African-American Athlete 1919-1945.* New York: Warner Books, 1988.

_____. A Hard Road to Glory: A History of the African-American Athlete Since 1946. New York: Warner Books, 1988.

Gibson, Althea. *I Always Wanted to Be Somebody.* New York: Harper & Brothers, 1958.

_____. *So Much to Live For.* New York: Putnam, 1968.

Grimsley, Will. *Tennis: Its History, People and Events.* Englewood Cliffs: Prentice-Hall, 1971.

Hollander, Phyllis. *American Women in Sports.* New York: Grosset & Dunlap, 1972.

King, Billie Jean. *We Have Come a Long Way.* New York: McGraw-Hill, 1988.

Lichtenstein, Grace. *A Long Way, Baby: Behind the Scenes in Women's Pro Tennis.* New York: Morrow, 1974.

Lumpkin, Angela. *Women's Tennis: A Historical Documentary of the Players and Their Game.* Troy, NY: Whitston Publications, 1981.

Ryan, Joan. *Contributions of Women: Sports.* Minneapolis: Dillon Press, 1975.

Sullivan, George. *Queens of the Court.* New York: Dodd, Mead, 1974.

CHRONOLOGY

1927   Althea Gibson born in Silver, South Carolina, August 25

1930   Moves to New York City

1941   Starts taking tennis lessons at Harlem's Cosmopolitan Club

1942   Enters and wins her first tournament, sponsored by the all-black American Tennis Association (ATA)

1946   Moves to Wilmington, North Carolina, to work on her tennis game with Dr. Hubert A. Eaton; enrolls in high school there

1947   Wins the first of ten straight ATA National Championships

1949   Competes against white players for the first time; enrolls at Florida A&M University in Tallahassee, Florida

1950   Enters her first outdoor United States Lawn Tennis Association (USLTA) tournaments; plays in the U.S. National Tennis Championships at Forest Hills

1951   Competes in the All-England Tennis Championships at Wimbledon for the first time

1953   Graduates from Florida A&M; moves to Jefferson City, Missouri 1954

1954   Starts working with tennis coach Sydney Llewellyn

1955-56   Travels throughout Southeast Asia on a U.S. State Department-sponsored goodwill tennis tour

1956   Wins the French Championships; tours the Australian tennis tournament circuit

1957   Wins the All-England Championships at Wimbledon and the U.S. National Tennis Championships at Forest Hills

1958   Wins Wimbledon and Forest Hills; retires from amateur tennis

1959	Releases a record album, *Althea Gibson Sings*; appears in a film, *The Horse Soldiers*
1960	Tours with the Harlem Globetrotters playing exhibition tennis
1964	Launches her professional golf career; joins the Ladies Professional Golf Association (LPGA)
1965	Marries Will Darben
1971	Retires from professional golf; starts a career as a professional tennis teacher
1975	Divorces Will Darben; takes a job as manager of the East Orange, New Jersey, Department of Recreation

PICTURE CREDITS

INDEX

Tom Biracree is the author of 35 books. A former high school coach and sportswriter, he lives with his wife, Nancy, and son, Ryan, in Ridgefield, Connecticut.

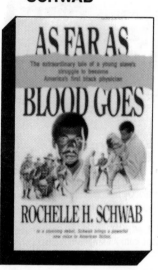

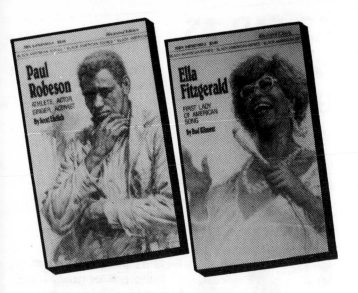

MELROSE SQUARE
BLACK AMERICAN SERIES

Melrose Square proudly announces a new series of Black American biographies. Each volume is profusely illustrated, meticulously researched, widely acclaimed. The first four titles are now available. Quality paperback format: $3.95 each.

PAUL ROBESON: ATHLETE, ACTOR, SINGER, ACTIVIST. Written by Scott Ehrlich, this is the story of the gifted man who went from All-American football player at Rutgers (where he graduated first in his class) to win worldwide respect as a performer.

ELLA FITZGERALD: FIRST LADY OF AMERICAN SONG. Written by Bud Kliment, this beautifully-told biography traces Ella's fascinating life from her birth in Virginia to her White House—and international—acclaim as America's "First Lady of Song."

NAT TURNER: PROPHET AND SLAVE LEADER. Written by Terry Bisson. Fiery preacher, militant leader—and prophet—Nat Turner organized a slave uprising that struck a defiant blow against slavery in the United States thirty years before the Civil War.

JACKIE ROBINSON: FIRST BLACK IN PROFESSIONAL BASEBALL. Written by Richard Scott. The story of the man who was good enough, professional enough and, most of all, man enough to be selected to break the "color barrier" in professional baseball.